IT'S HARD TO RUN IN A SARI

IT'S HARD TO RUN IN A SARI

PRIYA MARY SEBASTIAN

Cover Design by Vinaya Ann Alapatt

Copyrighted Material

It's Hard to Run in a Sari

Copyright © 2021 by Priya. All Rights Reserved.

No part of this publication may be reproduced, stored in a retrieval system or transmitted, in any form or by any means—electronic, mechanical, photocopying, recording or otherwise—without prior written permission from the publisher, except for the inclusion of brief quotations in a review.

For information about this title or to order other books and/or electronic media, contact the publisher:

Priya
Indiacafeaugusta.com
sebastianmary866@gmail.com

ISBNs:
978-1-7351228-3-0 (hardcover)
978-1-7351228-4-7 (softcover)
978-1-7351228-5-4 (eBook)

Printed in the United States of America

Cover: Vinaya Ann Alapatt
Cover and Interior design: 1106 Design

This book is lovingly dedicated to my dear children, Kavya and Arjun. I am amazed at your achievements and the confident clarity with which you deal with the world. I know you laugh when your mother refers to female physicians as "lady doctors," and you wonder why I get so nervous—even with GPS—when I drive into Atlanta alone. You roll your eyes when I meticulously put away food in little labeled containers for Dad, even when I leave to visit family in India. After forty-two years in this country I have never seen the inside of a bar, not out of any virtue, but because I just don't feel comfortable going to one. We are all products of the period we grew up in, with its particular quirks and idiosyncrasies. It shapes us into who we are, and even when we try to adapt and evolve with changing times, there is a core that is hardwired. So bear with me. Mom has changed in many ways to meet the challenges of the modern era, but in my heart of hearts, there is still a little girl who grew up in rural India in the '60s.

With my undying love and admiration,
~Mom

A NOTE FROM THE AUTHOR

Today, as I watch President Joe Biden give his State of the Union address and I look with pride at the two most powerful women in the country, Vice President Kamala Harris and Speaker of the House Nancy Pelosi, who are sitting behind him, I am filled with pride at the great strides women have made in the world.

In 2017, Air India's first all-female crew took a jetliner around the world, breaking a record. And this January, an all-female Indian pilot team made history by completing the longest non-stop commercial flight operated by an Indian national airline. The U.S. is considering equal wages for men and women, and I have a feeling that this will be a reality very soon.

This leads me to reflect on my own journey, one that started in India with my birth in the late 1950s. When I was growing up in India in the 1960s, it was understood that being a woman meant that you had major restrictions on your freedom. There were few places you could go alone, and most of the decisions in life, like the kind of education you could get, or when and whom you could marry, were all made by the so-called responsible male figures in your family. Anyone who dared to rebel would be deemed an outcast, forever looked at with scorn or pity.

I remember a great aunt who became an engineer; in fact, she became the chief engineer for the state of Kerala. But she paid a price: She remained single her whole life, and I am sure it was not by choice.

Women were groomed to be good housewives and mothers, and obedience to authority figures (mostly male) was emphasized. Naturally, this narrow-minded thinking extended to marriage. Marriages were arranged without consulting the bride, and the only concern was that the groom should be from the same religion, caste, and socio-economic background.

In India in those days, the opposite of the arranged marriage was the love marriage, when two people from different backgrounds sometimes dared to fall in love, and, defying all social obstacles thrown their way, managed to tie the knot. Many a time, they were permanently alienated from their families and missed the easy familiarity of social occasions. Those (and their children) who dared to defy the ancient dictates of society bore this stigma like a permanent tattoo.

You can only imagine the social ostracizing when estrangement or divorce came into the picture. Back then, only a few movie stars (the most avant-garde of society) got divorced. But when they did, it was almost always done secretly, so nobody learned of it.

When we hear that in certain Gulf countries women are not allowed to go out in public, even to a supermarket by themselves, we are outraged. But I can remember in the '60s in India, women had to be accompanied by a male figure when they ventured outside of their homes, sometimes even to walk to a college.

In that sense the poorest women had the greatest freedom. They walked to their place of employment, usually as domestic help, as a field hand, or as a worker in a factory, and no one bothered them. Due to sheer necessity, their income, however meager, was a welcome relief to their households; it meant they could put food on the table for that day. Even then, the money was usually controlled by their husbands, some of whom would use it to drink themselves into oblivion.

Yet some women dared to dream and defy social norms. In the '70s and '80s they became secretaries, teachers, doctors, salesgirls, and other professionals who worked and earned a living. Other women dared to marry outside their communities, incurring the everlasting wrath of the patriarchal hierarchy, and bravely suffering social isolation.

That was where and when an avalanche started, one now speeding up with a momentum of its own, carving its own path as it crushes the shackles that have bound women for far too long.

CONTENTS

A Note from the Author	vii
Chapter 1	1
Chapter 2	11
Chapter 3	19
Chapter 4	24
Chapter 5	30
Chapter 6	36
Chapter 7	44
Chapter 8	48
Chapter 9	52
Chapter 10	58
Chapter 11	62
Chapter 12	69
Chapter 13	73
Chapter 14	83

Chapter 15	88
Chapter 16	95
Chapter 17	103
Chapter 18	108
Chapter 19	115
Chapter 20	121
Chapter 21	128
Chapter 22	135
Chapter 23	143
Chapter 24	151
Chapter 25	158
Chapter 26	167
Chapter 27	173
Chapter 28	183
Chapter 29	195
Chapter 30	205
Acknowledgments	213
About the Author	217

CHAPTER 1

The year was 1950. Lakshmi was born in the inner room of her maternal grandparents' home in the little village of Karukutty, India. Her grandfather, a man in his fifties, paced outside on the *ummeram* (veranda), his hands clasped behind him in a state of nervous anxiety. The painful cries of Nalini, the young Hindu mother going through the birthing ritual, the most primordial of all human functions, echoed throughout the house. She was attended by her mother, Janakiamma, grandmother, Narayaniamma, and the village midwife. You could hear the grandmother instructing her younger counterparts: "Kuttikkithiri vellam kodukku chundu nanakkaan." ("Give the girl a little water to wet her lips.")

Nalini had been ceremonially brought to her parents' home for the three-month period of the confinement. In the days when maternal and infant mortality rates were high, it was believed that the expectant mother would feel most at ease in her childhood home, attended to by her mother—as opposed to her in-laws.

It was perhaps also an attempt to keep the woman away from the sexual advances of an overly zealous husband, which, it was believed, might harm the baby.

For Nalini's Seemantham ceremony (a ritual similar to a Western baby shower, carried out during the sixth to eighth month of pregnancy), the ladies rubbed herbal oil on Nalini and gave her a ritual bath. They put flowers in her hair and adorned her like a new bride, with bangles glinting and jingling on her hands. Then, for good luck, they placed *unniyappams* (rice cakes made of pounded rice and jaggery, or coarse brown sugar) and rice grains in her lap.

The village *Ayurvedic* (native herbal doctor) was consulted. He prescribed a bevy of *kozhambus* (herbal oils) and *kashaayams* (bitter herbal medicines thought to cure blood impurities), and explained the order in which these were to be taken to ensure a safe delivery for mother and child. He also prescribed a mainly vegetarian diet so that the patient's gastric systems were not overly taxed.

The older female relatives who came to visit or to attend the Seemantham enjoyed making sage-like pronouncements: "Kutteede mughathe eishwaryam kanditte, penkuttiyaavumennaa thonnane." ("Seeing how beautiful the mother has become, I feel it is going to be a girl.") Another proclaimed that since Nalini's stomach had a pointed look, this was a sure indication of a boy. Nalini's mother and grandmother had beamed at this suggestion.

This was a world of women. They were seeing yet another woman through one of life's greatest, yet most treacherous, moments. This was a sanctuary where men were not welcome, and their services were required only if, heaven forbid, a dire emergency occurred. Given that this was a home delivery, should complications arise, the family would have to call a taxi, wait for it to arrive and take Nalini and her mother to the nearest hospital, and hope it was not too late!

Most men were notified when their wives gave birth, and they would arrive formally to see the baby within the next couple of days. It was the rare father who would even attempt to hold his own child.

The woman would stay at her maternal home for three months after the delivery to recuperate. She would then be ceremonially escorted back to her married home by her husband and his family.

✺

The moaning from the room intensified, and at last was mixed with the shrill cry of a little person making her way into the vast universe. The midwife officially carried the baby to its mother. As she placed the baby in Nalini's arms, you could hear the apologetic note in her voice as she said, "Penkuttiaa, pakshe magam perannathaane." ("It's a girl . . . but she is born in the month of Magam, which is auspicious for girls.")

"Lakshmikutty" ("Baby Lakshmi") her mother called her— and that was the name! While the midwife cleaned up the new mother, the grandmother went outside to inform the grandfather. "Vegam oru telegram adikkanam, Shankarane ariyikkande." ("We need to send a telegram immediately to inform Shankaran.")

A messenger was dispatched to the local post office to send a telegram to Lakshmi's father, who was working in another town, informing him of his daughter's birth, but with as few words as possible to save money. It read: "Girl born 11.10 a.m." The timing to the exact minute was crucial—this was the information the *Panikkar* (astrologer) would use to mark the twists and turns Lakshmi's young life would take from now until the end of her days.

After an hour, when every vestige of the human struggle that had just taken place had been erased and the room was set to order, Lakshmi's grandfather visited for the first time.

He took one look at the exhausted but smiling mother and picked up the baby from its little *Attuthottil* (rocking baby cradle). It had been in the family for generations; its sturdy wooden construction had soothed many a baby to a gentle sleep. "Lakshanamulla mughaane," her grandfather opined. ("She has a good face.")

"Athine nammada kutteede mughalle," the grandmother, standing behind him, chimed in. ("But then, it is our granddaughter's face.") She was more than a little proud that her female progeny had inherited her good looks.

She then helped the midwife fold lengths of fabric into a thick girdle to tie around the new mother's stomach so the muscles that had been expanded in childbirth would slowly contract.

Karthiyani, who worked in the kitchen, was hurriedly called to take out the *chaavupilla* (placenta) and bury it outside in a deep ditch so that no animal could get at it. That would be most inauspicious.

Little Lakshmi suckled heartily at her mother's breasts, the only universe she was cognizant of at this point. She ate and slept, unaware of the wheels that had been set in motion the minute she was born.

The old lady who specialized in giving baths to new mothers, as well as their babies, was called into service. Her frame was bent from picking up many a newborn to give them their first luxurious bath. She first rubbed the mother down with coconut oil infused with tulsi leaves and peppercorns (which were

CHAPTER 1

supposed to ward off colds and flus), and then massaged her hair with more of the same oil.

In her gnarled hands, she gathered a bunch of reeds, bruised them, and made a herbal broom called *thaali,* to produce a soap-like substance used to cleanse the hair. On the body she used *shikkakkai* (soapnut) powder and meticulously checked the water temperature. (Everything had to be perfect for the complete recovery of the mother after childbirth—and the bath woman was a thorough professional, after all.)

She bathed Nalini, taking care to massage her breasts to produce more milk, and also massaged her stomach muscles to help them return to their original youthful shape. Once Nalini was safely ensconced on her birthing bed, it was the baby's turn.

A rectangular piece of raised wood a bit bigger than the baby was used. It had a patina borne from years of use in the family to bathe infants, where oil and water had mingled to give the wood a natural soothing softness. Lakshmi was ceremoniously laid out on this piece of wood.

While taking off the baby's loincloth, held together by a black thick thread around her tiny waist, the old woman crooned, "Ende kuttikke kulikkande, sundarikutty aavande." ("Don't you want a bath? Don't you want to look all pretty?")

The baby gurgled and kicked. The squatting woman rubbed her with the special oil. She took care to manipulate the features of the child into the best they could be. She massaged the nose to make it more aquiline and tried to shape the head into a rounder, more desirable shape, rather than a newborn's elongated shape. She even manipulated the ears to open them up. The newborn's legs and hands were stretched so that she would not be cursed with bowlegs.

When these tasks were complete, she gently bathed the baby in lukewarm water and turned her over in the palm of her hand to bathe the little one's profuse hair. At this point, little Lakshmi had had enough, and she let out a wail.

The old lady soothed Lakshmi: "Saarallya kutty, the' kazhinju, kuttikkini poyi mamam unnaalo." ("It is all finished, now baby can eat her food.")

Lakshmi gorged herself at her mother's breasts then lay contented on the bed surrounded by round pillows. Her eyes were lined with kohl and her mother strategically placed a big dark spot of kohl on her chin to ward off any evil eye. Her toothless gummy mouth occasionally smiled involuntarily; she was oblivious to the big decisions affecting her life being made by the adults outside on the veranda.

❈

The Panikkar was hastily summoned. He squatted on the floor of the veranda and spread out the tools of his trade: some dried palm leaves, a nail to etch the horoscope on them, and chalk to draw checkerboard patterns on the floor and arrange the planetary positions on it. The rest was in his head, in the form of verses memorized from childhood as to the possible outcomes when the planets were in certain positions. It was and is a trade passed on from generation to generation in an unbroken chain.

He assigned the planets their positions inside the neat little squares. With the exact time of birth, he predicted little Lakshmi's future, scraped in the small confines of a palm leaf with a nail. The astrologer scratched his head and hesitated. The others on the veranda waited anxiously.

"Kuttikke korache chowwadosham kaninde." ("I see a little problem with a predominant presence of Mars"), began the astrologer apologetically. He worried that his remuneration would take a hit if the outcome was unfavorable. But the integrity of his profession would not allow him to let this major flaw in the reading go unmentioned. There was a collective exhaling of breath, as if the air in a balloon had been set free.

The grandmother pleaded with the astrologer: "Onnu koodi nokku Pannikare, valla thettum patteettudonne,kalyaana samayaavumba velia budhimuttaaville." ("Please look once more, astrologer, because otherwise it will cause a lot of difficulty during the time of marriage.")

A child with the Chowwadosham configuration in their astrological chart was not likely to make a good marriage. One could argue that a predominance of the planet Mars would give one a cantankerous nature—definitely not conducive to a marriage. This problem was usually solved by arranging a marriage where the bride and the groom both have Chowwadosham in their respective horoscopes, thus cancelling out the curse.

But it was always a problem that created headaches for parents and grandparents. The Panikkar braved the irritations of the elders and stuck to his guns. The girl definitely had Cowwadosham in her *jaathakam* (astrology).

The grandfather reluctantly took out a ₹50 note, which the astrologer accepted in both hands, touching it to his forehead. Apologetically, he collected his paraphernalia and prepared to leave, murmuring, "Njanendaa cheyya? Ollathalle parayaan pattoo?" ("What am I supposed to do? I can only say what is written in the stars.") He made a hasty exit.

The Panikker's words weighed heavily on everyone. After supper that evening, the grandfather lounged in his easy chair while the grandmother sat beside him on a stool. She took out an ancient brass box containing betel leaves, *chunnaambe* (lime), and arecnuts. She carefully removed each leaf, making sure to pinch off the stem. Then she liberally applied the lime paste and placed a small piece of arecnut in the center of each leaf, which she folded several times to make it look like a little purse. She handed it to the grandfather, who placed it in his mouth. After more than fifty years of marriage, this was about the only act of intimacy they had between them. He chewed on the leaves with satisfaction, expressed with a loud clearing of his throat.

The grandmother leaned over. She whispered, "Mattennaale, Sankaranum avande achanum ammemm kuttiye kaanaan varille! Kuttikke kazhuthilekkum, kayyilekkum vallathum vende?" ("Day after tomorrow, Shankaran and his parents will come to see the baby. Don't you think we need to adorn little Lakshmi's hands and neck with some ornaments?")

In the well-to-do families, it was and is customary for the maternal grandparents to provide the child, even a boy child, with a couple of gold bangles, a gold chain, a gold waist chain (to hang the cloth diaper from), and gold anklets.

It is also a tradition to send basket loads of goodies like sharkaravaratti (fried plantain nuggets coated with jaggery), banana chips, *kalkals* (fried pastry) and other sweet and savory items to the in-laws, where the mother-in-law has the privilege of distributing it to their relatives, thus announcing the birth of the grandchild.

The grandfather leaned back heavily in his easy chair. As a retired government clerk, he was the recipient of a ₹2000-a-month pension. Most of his savings had gone to marry off Nalini and educate her brother, who had finished his bachelor's in commerce and was working in a bank. The price of gold was ₹800 for a

CHAPTER 1

sovereign. He had only to do some mental math to figure out the dent this customary visit from the in-laws would cost him.

But he was not one to shy away from his responsibilities. The next day the grandparents visited the local jewellry store. The grandmother brought along a couple of her bangles and an old necklace given to her by her parents. She exchanged all this, along with some money, for two tiny little bangles, a small chain, an *aranjaanam* (waist chain) and anklets for the tiny feet.

When the in-laws visited, little Lakshmi was laid out in all her finery. Her father stood near the bed, beaming at his new daughter, a little embarrassed to pick her up.

His mother had no such problems. She scooped up the baby and cooed, "Ithaaraa, Lakshmikuttikke ammoomme manassilaayo?" ("Who is this little girl, do you recognize your grandmother, little Lakshmi?") She wasted no time voicing her opinion about the newborn's appearance either. "Mugham tharakkedilla, pakshe ente Shankarante neram onnum kitteettillatto." ("Her face is all right, but she certainly did not get my son Shankaran's fair complexion.")

Nalini and her mother, Janakiamma, cringed. The visitors sit down to a good spread prepared by the grandmother and the great-grandmother, who stood by ingratiatingly, making sure that the guests were served first and later, plying them with even more food.

The guests had said their goodbyes and left when Lakshmi decided to throw the first temper tantrum of her young life. "Weeeh, weeeh, weeh!"—she let herself be known, much to the consternation of Nalini and her mother. They were in a state trying to figure out if the child had colic or whether she was just plain hungry! Such was the fanfare that heralded the birth of little Lakshmi into this world.

Her grandmother made a mixture of honey, *vayambe* (native herb) and gold (usually a piece of gold rubbed on a coarse stone; a bit of the fine dust is gathered for this purpose), and put a few drops on little Lakshmi's tongue, so the child would acquire a great complexion. The baby did not like it. She made a distasteful face.

Lakshmi's mother, Nalini, grew up in a joint family where her parents were also taking care of her aging grandparents. So Lakshmi's birth was witnessed by three generations. On the twenty-eighth day, she was placed in her great-grandfather's lap, and he formally named her. "Lakshmikutty," he repeated three times in her ear, and the child looked up, startled.

CHAPTER 2

"*Ayyo, njaan veene ponu, patheke!*" ("Oh no, I am falling off, go slowly!")

Lakshmi shrieked as her brother pulled her around the sharp bend near the ditch of the coconut tree. She was sitting cross-legged in a makeshift sleigh made of a palm frond with the leaves attached. She hung on for dear life to the neck of the frond that connected it to the long leaves. Her brother grasped the tip of the leaves as he ran, taking her for a bumpy ride over sand dunes, tree branches, and sharp stones. It was a game they never tired of.

Did I forget to mention that Lakshmi's mother, Nalini, had once more gone through the rigors of childbirth? This time it was a boy! Balan's birth, three years after Lakshmi's, was accompanied by even more fanfare than his sister's. This time, the old grandfather did not seem to mind that he had to touch his meager pensions again. Grandmother made *paayasam* (a sweet vermicelli pudding prepared for every auspicious event). It was distributed to all nearby homes along with the good news that Nalini was delivered of a healthy baby boy!

This time, the in-laws came bearing gifts for the little prince. Even the mother-in-law relented a little to announce: "Nalla eishwaryolla kuttiyaa, nalla face cut." ("He has a noble face and great facial features.") Lakshmi's mother and grandmother nodded in agreement, smiling broadly. By now the great-grandfather was no more, and even the great-grandmother was confined to a chair because of weakness. But she was smiling her toothless smile, happy that the gods had blessed them with a male child.

Even Lakshmi's father, Shankaran, who had never picked up an infant, awkwardly picked up Balan and twirled him around, saying, "Ente mon enne vayasukaalathe nokkille?" ("Won't my son look after me in my old age?") When the baby made a contented noise, Shankaran took that as Balan's promise to him.

After the traditional three-month rest and recuperation following childbirth, Nalini returned to the little two-bedroom rented house in Kodakara where Shankaran worked as a clerk/bookkeeper for a furniture store.

The Panikkar (astrologer) had predicted that Balan would be a scholar and later, an important officer. For his troubles, the Panikkar had been suitably reimbursed. He left the little family group on the veranda beaming at each other in anticipation of the great events he had foretold.

❖

Lakshmi was now eight years old and Balan had just turned five. Amma (mother) called out from the veranda: "Lakshmikutty, kalichathe mathi, poyi kulichu velakku koluthi naamam chelle. Penkuttiyolude oru kali!" ("Lakshmi, that is enough of playing.

CHAPTER 2

Go take a bath, light the lamp in the prayer room and recite your prayers. The way these girls are playing nowadays!")

Lakshmi tried to protest; they were just getting the hang of the game and could pull the palm leaf without tipping the other person out of it. Nalini had to choose that time to call her out. She was peeved and registered her complaint: "Appo Balan porathalle?" ("But Balan is playing outside?") At the little girl's cheek, her mother bristled. "Thonnyaasam parayaande keri ponundo? Ende kayyeenne onnu vaangikum! Penkuttiyolde oru ahangaaram." ("Are you coming inside without mouthing off or not? You are going to get a smack from me! Little girls these days are so full of themselves.")

Lakshmi knew there was no more argument to be made. She walked back to the house in quiet resignation, but not before throwing a resentful, blazing look towards Balan, who was already onto his next game—jumping in and out of the ditches dug around the coconut trees. These fairly deep trenches were designed to hold the water and fertilizer for the tree. Sometimes during Chaakara season, when the oceans are so full of sardines that they go to waste (because of lack of refrigeration), they are dumped by the basketful into these trenches. She was furious, especially when Balan grinned at her and stuck out his tongue behind their mother's back.

✺

It was seven in the morning, and the entire household was up and about.

Lakshmi was a bright child; she loved school. She liked getting ready for it by braiding her hair. Long and dark, it glistened with coconut oil as she wove it into one long braid with a ribbon at the end. She would cover her face with talcum powder, carefully looking into the small mirror on the wall in her parents' room. She would touch up her brows and, with an eyebrow pencil, draw her eyes out in the shape of a fish. She had seen the Malayalam movie stars Sheela and Sharada dressed up like this, using their eyes expressively to convey happiness, sorrow, horror, or even flirtation.

Lakshmi had plucked some of the little jasmine flowers that opened on a bush every morning. They looked like little snowflakes in a sea of green with the morning dew still fresh upon them. Using a needle and thread, she strung them into a garland to be worn in her hair, pinned into place with a hairpin.

She and Balan sat at the small Formica dining table and Amma put steaming plates of *idlis* (a rice cake) and chutney in front of them. "Vegam kazhikkoo, rickshaw ippo ethum." ("Eat quickly, the rickshaw will be here soon.") Shortly, you could hear the bell of the cycle rickshaw driving up. Four kids sat inside and two hung on by the foot boards! There was still room for two more to be cramped inside. "Ellaavarum onne othunghi irunne," the rickshawwalla would urge the children. ("Everyone please sit as compactly as possible.")

Nalini straightened the children's hair and placed a small lunch pack in each of their book bags. This was a small steel container that held a little rice and *aviyal* (a mixed vegetable curry). They would drink and wash their hands with water from the school well.

The rickshaw driver grinned at Lakshmi, and with the smugness of his authority and an air befitting his responsibility, he announced to Nalini, "Naale Kaashe tharanam, saadhanangalkokke enthaa vela." ("I need the rickshaw fares tomorrow. Boy, are things getting expensive or what?") With that he climbed

CHAPTER 2

onto his seat, shifted his weight to balance the load behind, and off they went, bumping along the ditches on the road with the kids chattering and laughing behind.

❈

Ammoomma (grandmother) was visiting when Lakshmi came of age at thirteen. Her great-grandmother had also passed away in her sleep. Now that her grandmother had dutifully taken care of her parents till they died, she had a little free time to visit her grandkids. As if the embarrassment of your private parts suddenly coming to life was not bad enough, Ammoomma had to announce it to the whole village! Any relative or friend of the family who came by the house, whether a man or a woman, Ammoomma proudly informed them, "Nammade Lakshmikutty vayasariyichu!" ("Our Lakshmi has come of age!")

She might as well have taken a *parasyam* (advertisement) in the local paper in big, bold letters. Better still, it could have been like the lottery announcement from a car with a loudspeaker attached to the roof: "Kerala bhaagyakury, vegam vaanguga, onnaam sammaanam 10 laksham roopa!" ("Kerala lottery tickets for sale! Come and get it quickly, the first prize, 10 lakh rupees!") Ammoomma's announcement proceeded along the lines of, "Laksmikkutti vayasariyichirikanu! ellavarum kelkkuga." ("Lakshmi has come of age! Hear ye, hear ye.")

Lakshmi could not understand what all the fuss was about. She was embarrassed by the way her brother and his friends, whom she had played with just the previous day, looked at her with leering grins, like they were aware that her status had changed. No more was she allowed to go out and play *kutty and kole* (the two-stick game) with them. And once or twice, when she ran out of the house to join them, Nalini's voice was sharp with disapproval when she called her back. "Kuttikkali kaliche nadakkanda praayam okke kazhinju. Ini ivide veettil adangi othungi irunna matheetto." ("The days of playing little kid games are over for you. It is best if you confined yourself to the house from now on.")

Lakshmi's whole world had changed. But as much a she hated the new limitations placed on her, she felt a certain excitement at her new status. Her mother ripped apart some of old cotton sarees, then showed Lakshmi how to dress herself during these inconvenient times. She would use the cotton pads as a loincloth hung from the black strong thread she wore around her waist.

It was a chore to wash and hang them up from the clothesline strung from one coconut tree to another. And if any of the boys were playing in the ditches, they would nudge each other and look her way, giving knowledgeable grins. Lakshmi could feel her face grow hot in embarrassment.

Ammoomma's sleeping pallet was next to hers. Ammoomma would tell her stories of virtuous women who would defend their men and protect their virtue even in the most trying of times. On a full moon night, the old lady would sit on her pallet, gather her sparse stringy hair (it smelled of coconut oil) into a small knot on the top of her head and inform Lakshmi: "Inne poornanilaavaa! Yakshiyole erangi nadakkindaavum! Praayam vanna penkuttiyole kamizhnne kedakkanam, yakshi kaananda. Pidichonde povum." ("Today is a full moon night, that's when all the nightly spirits start walking around. It is best that girls who have come of age lie face down, so that the spirits don't see them and take them away.") The thought was a little unnerving, and Lakshmi dutifully lay on her stomach.

CHAPTER 2

Just like in the western countries where little kids were told stories of Red Riding Hood and Hansel and Gretel, every culture tries its best to protect its young from the clutches of evil.

Lakshmi now noticed that attentions were coming her way—both wanted and unwanted. She was more than a little pleased when, one day while walking alone to school hugging her books to her chest, Gopi from next door rode by on his bicycle. With his black hair a little too long and his smile a little too cheeky, he solicitously inquired of her: "Lakshmikutteene schoolee kondu vidatte? Ivide kerikkolu." ("Lakshmi, shall I take you to school, just hop on here.") He pointed to the handlebar in front of him, meaning she was to ride sidesaddle with him like in the movies.

There were some unwanted attentions as well. As Lakshmi and her friends were walking towards school, they passed a two-story house painted in bright colours. Her friend Divya said, "Athoru gulf kaarante veeda. Ummem kuttiyolum ivideya." ("That house belongs to a guy who works in the Gulf. His wife and children live there.") One day, a tall, fair gentleman in his mid-thirties came out of the gate in a *lunghi* (a colourful dhoti, or type of sarong). Seeing the girls, he leaned against the wall with a suggestive smile. "Ellaarum nannaayitte padikanundo? Doctor aavumbo enne chikilsikkanam ketto." ("Are all of you studying well? When you become doctors, you need to treat me, okay?")

They walked a little faster with their heads down. This drew even more mirth from their tormentor. When they were out of earshot, Divya whispered fiercely, "Olla orennam poraandaano ineem nokkane, pinne venda kaashundallo, randum, moonnum okke avaallo." ("Isn't he satisfied with the one wife he already has, or is he looking for more? I guess he has enough money; it can be two or three, I suppose.") She meant the beautiful lady they had seen looking out of the window of the house, the tip of her pink sari draped like a veil over her head and little gold loops running all the way up her ears. They felt a kinship with this beautiful heroine who had to contend with her Romeo with the wandering eye.

CHAPTER 3

"*Lakshmi chechi, ee kanakke enthoru budhimutta!* Onnu paranju thanne," demanded little Balan, now ten, in his usual imperious way. ("Lakshmi, big sister, this math is so difficult. Come and help me!")

He knew that everyone in the household lived to fulfill his every wish. He was spoilt and playful and failing math. This prompted his parents to hire the services of Mr. Iyer, a retired Brahmin schoolteacher who lived and breathed math.

Balan hated him, and he whined when he saw Mr. Iyer walk towards the house for his six o'clock lesson. But this was one sacred area where his parents refused to cave in to his wishes.

Lakshmi on the other hand, was good at her studies and especially enjoyed the challenges of mathematics. She would quiz her brother: "The Madras mail travels between Coimbatore and Madras at a speed of 50 mph. It stops at the Salem Junction for about ten minutes. It started out from Coimbatore at 10:00

p.m. and the distance from Coimbatore to Madras is 200 km. When did the train arrive in Madras?"

Balan was stuck. Lakshmi patiently explained how to calculate the distance covered at 50 mph and the time deducted for when the train was inactive. "Kandille Baalaa, ithu easy alle?" ("See, Balan, it is fairly easy.") Balan gave her a stormy look. After jotting down the answer he closed his notebook with a dramatic thud and ran off to play football (soccer) with his buddies.

Lakshmi went back to her history book. It was the only subject she found tiresome because of all the dates she had to remember and reproduce. She read while walking up and down the length of the small veranda. "Emperor Ashoka planted trees all along the main roads for the comfort of the travellers. He also dug a lot of wells for the weary travellers to drink. The great Emperor was so enlightened that he even married women who were not from the same religion."

Her mother poked her irritated face through the door. She grumbled, "Ashokan vellia kaaryangale cheythathonde ente ari vevilla! Kutty poi kenateenne ithiri vellam kori konduvanne ari kazhuki ide." ("For all the great things Emperor Ashoka did, it is not going to cook my rice! Get some water from the well, wash the rice for me, and put it in the pot for cooking.") Her mother's aspirations for her daughter were more of the earth.

❃

It was tenth grade and final exams were coming. Some girls were already dreaming of going to local colleges by bus and pursuing their education. Others, those who were less motivated or could not afford it, would attend local parallel colleges. These were no more than a shed with a chalkboard and high school-level teachers, many retired.

CHAPTER 3

Lakshmi harbored a secret dream. She would be a high school math teacher like Shailaja teacher, her high school math teacher. She would go to school wearing beautiful colourful sarees with a *bindi* (a coloured dot worn in the middle of the forehead) and a dab of sandalwood paste on her forehead. When she entered her classroom, the students would rise and chorus, "Good morning, Lakshmi teacher!"

She envisioned concerned parents lining up outside her classroom. She would queue them up in the order of arrival. Then, one by one, at her command, they would enter the sacred sanctum of her classroom and approach her desk with the timidity of three-year-olds.

"Ente Jaanakeede karyam anweshikkaan vannathaa, teacheravalode nannaayi padikkaan parayanam. Thotte thoppiyittirikka." ("I have come to inquire about the progress of our daughter Jaanaki. Teacher, you need to tell her to pay more attention to her studies. She has failed in so many tests.")

Lakshmi teacher would give a knowledgeable nod and a sympathetic smile. She would exhort them to renew their efforts in making sure that Jaanaki did her work and, if necessary, punish her a little bit (after all, no child has ever died because of a few licks of the cane on the inside of their hand), so she would stick to the straight and narrow. Thus reassured, the parents would thank her profusely. The mother would even attempt to touch Lakshmi's feet in her mountain of gratitude, which Lakshmi would magnanimously prevent her from doing. Still bowing, hands together in a pose of supplication, the duo would make their exit.

"Next," Lakshmi would call from her privileged chair behind the desk, and the next trembling souls would enter the halls of this deity. And on and on it went. This private dream was re-embellished with each version.

At fifteen, Lakshmi wrote the statewide S.S.L.C exam, which every tenth grader had to pass to finish school. The exam was administered in another school so there would be no foul play by the students to boost their scores.

It was the first time Lakshmi carried a Hall ticket, an official document with her picture and her carefully thought-out signature (with a flourish at the end). On it was written the most important piece of information—her ID number. She was required to show this document to be allowed into the exam hall and then, without making a single mistake, copy the number onto the exam sheet. This would ensure that the person correcting the papers would have no idea whose paper it was.

It was a system devised before the age of computers. Take into consideration the extreme competition to get into professional colleges in a country teeming with young people, and you can understand why they were adept at trying to cut a few corners by bribing—or outright bullying—those who corrected the papers into giving better grades than deserved.

On the day the results were printed in the newspapers, with much trepidation and a quick prayer in the *puja* (prayer) room, Lakshmi and her parents looked for her number. Lakshmi gave a whoop of joy. "The' ende numbare, haavu, paassaayi!" ("My number is right here. Whew! I passed.") Her mother and grandmother rejoiced with her and reminded her that they had always been sure she would pass.

Those who passed proudly trooped to the school to claim their mark books and get their graduation certificates. As for the unfortunate souls who failed, they were not heard from again. You could find them in the fields and the construction sites grumbling about a system that set them up for a hard life.

Lakshmi's friend Divya stood next to her as they opened their mark books. "Enikku verum pass, ninakkenda," Divya asked. ("I just got a regular pass, what is your grade like?")

Lakshmi had to look a couple of times at the thin little book containing her earthly achievement to make sure that what she saw was no illusion. She had a first-class! It is a mark of distinction that sets apart the top 20 percent of the students.

As they were digesting this information, Shailaja teacher came towards them, beaming. She affectionately patted Lakshmi on the back and congratulated her. "You have the highest grade in the whole school for math; I told you that you were good at it!"

Lakshmi walked on air as she made her way back to her house.

CHAPTER 4

"*Acha, Amme enikke claassunde,* Shailaja teacher *parayanathe, collegilokke poyi vellia aalaavumbo njangale onnum marakkaruthenne.*" ("Dad, Mom, I passed with a first-class! Shailaja teacher teased me, saying that when I become an important person after a college education, I should not forget them.")

Lakshmi could barely get the words out. At fifteen, this was her first major achievement. She was so excited that she ran back from school after learning the S.S.L.C results.

She said to her parents, "Everyone says that St. Joseph's College in Irinjalakuda is really good and it is only a bus ride away. I could come back every evening and still have time for the chores around the house and my studying. Parvathy did not even have a first-class, and she is thinking of going there. She is taking chemistry because her father told her it was a practical subject."

Lakshmi campaigned hard. In her household, with her father's limited income as a bookkeeper in a furniture store,

CHAPTER 4

it was not a foregone conclusion that she would get to go to a real college. Her parents looked at each other (obviously they had given it some consideration in their private hours) with a certain sadness, borne out of the need to make hard choices. They certainly were aware that Lakshmi had potential and that she was a good student, and given the right encouragement, she had what it took to get somewhere.

In the wee hours of the night, as Nalini and Shankaran sat on their hard bed in the little room that was their private world, they went over it in their minds and in their hearts a thousand times. "Vellia collegile tuition koodum, pinne bus kooli, ithellaam kazhinje pennine kettichayakkande? Appo streedhanom kaaryangalum! Pennine padippe koodiyaale chekkane kittaanum veshamam aavum. Enthaa cheyya." ("In big colleges the tuition will be higher, not to mention the cost of bus transportation. And after all that, we will still have to marry her off and need to come up with a dowry. And if the girl is highly educated, it will be that much harder to get a groom who will be suitable for her.") As these conflicting thoughts raced through their minds, pragmatism—the usual go-to of all traditional low-income families, prevailed.

The next morning, Amma was serving hot, steaming plates of *puttu* (cylindrical-shaped steamed rice cakes garnished with grated coconut). The sweet smell of freshly grated coconut wafted through the air. This, along with some *kadala* (Bengal gram) curry and some steamed ripe plantains, was Lakshmi's favorite breakfast.

When Lakshmi sat down to eat, her father did not look up from his plate. She threw him a few furtive glances to gauge his mood. Shankaran was arranging in his mind how he could offer a fig leaf to his daughter without disappointing her too much, yet with an eye towards her future. Nalini lurked nearby, under the pretext of carrying dishes back and forth from the kitchen, serving newly made batches of puttu and plantains to everyone.

Everyone, including ten-year-old Balan, was aware that an important decision was coming down from Shankaran, as the head of the family, and it would have lasting effects on Lakshmi's life.

"Innale njaan bussine kaathe nikkumba, aa parallel collegee padippikkana teachere, nammade Menon sarille,varunu. Appo njangale kore neram samsaarichu. Ayaalu parenathe, parallel collegeennum kuttiyole nannaayi paassaavundenna." ("Yesterday, as I was waiting for my bus, I saw Mr. Menon, who teaches at the parallel college, and we talked for quite a bit of time. He was telling me that many kids who attend the parallel college attain their degrees just as easily as in regular colleges.")

Lakshmi knew where this conversation was heading. And as young as she was, she knew the difference between a higher institution of learning and a makeshift alternative, one for people who lacked the motivation, the means, or both. She could not hide her disappointment that her efforts had amounted to so little.

"Even Shailaja teacher told me that I had a bright future in mathematics and that I should study as much as I can in a good college. She said I would make a great teacher." Lakshmi blurted this out in despair, seeing the walls close in.

Her father replied, "Easy enough for Shailaja teacher to make such grand pronouncements! She is not paying for it, is she? And all that education—what good did it do her? A dried-up spinster with no husband and no family and not even a son to light her funeral pyre! That is what her education got her."

CHAPTER 4

Shankaran almost spat out the words, defensiveness creeping into his voice.

Lakshmi ran crying to the washstand to wash her hands, her half-eaten breakfast left at the table, like dreams discarded when one wakes up. Her Amma called after her, "Kutti onne kekke, ithum college thanneyalle, ividem padiche paassaavaallo, ingane veshamikkaanenthirikane" ("Girl, please listen, this is also college, and you can graduate from a parallel college too. There is no need to fret so much.")

To Amma, a high school dropout, even attending a parallel college seemed like a great leap forward. At least they were not asking Lakshmi to take sewing classes like the young women who lacked the money or the ability to attend college, or, like some lost souls, who lacked both. These unfortunate young women studied sewing and were lucky if they made a little money while waiting to be married.

Lakshmi's frustration spilled over into everything she did that summer. She did not talk much to her parents. When they tried to engage her in conversation, they received curt, one-word replies. She did her usual mundane chores around the house—drawing water from the well, sweeping the grounds in front of the house with a small, stout broom, and cutting up vegetables for Amma to make curries.

But she did it all with an air of martyrdom like she had seen the heroines in the movies do. When *Velliamma's* (older aunt's) children stayed with them for a few days during the summer vacation, at first Lakshmi would not talk to them.

She was a more intellectual human being than those stupid airheads, who thought only about the latest ways to comb their hair and colour their nails! She had bigger pursuits in life than getting married, and she believed no one understood or sympathized with her feelings and ambitions.

She heard Amma sitting on the bed in her room telling Velliamma in a worried tone, "Parallel collegee poyaa matheenne paranjappa thodangeethaa. Ee deshyom, mindaattom okke, enthaa cheyyaa? Namakke pattane malayalle chomakkaan pattoo." ("This started when we told her that we could send her only to the parallel college. This anger and silence, what can we do? We can only carry the mountains we are capable of.")

Poor Velliamma nodded in sympathetic assent and with more than a little bewilderment, because her two placid girls were happy not to be pushed too hard in education—or anything else in life. They were content to polish their nails and wait their turn for a chance to please a Prince Charming, one who would surely enter their lives at a nod from their parents.

But youth is a resilient state. With the persistent nagging of Balan and her two cousins, Lakshmi's resolve to become a martyr for life slowly dissolved. She found herself immersed in their games of hopscotch, bathing in the pond, catching butterflies (only to let them go), and little roundtable conferences under the coconut tree, sitting on the sandy soil and talking about life in general and movies and heroes in particular.

She soon forgot that she had suffered one of the biggest disappointments in her young life and raced around the yard trying to catch her younger cousin in a vigorous game of "catch the thief." At mealtimes, the children ate first. They sat in a circle on the floor and the women served them. They made so much noise with their animated chatter and arguments about who had won in the last game they played that Amma would gently chide them, "Ithrem ocha vekkathirikku. Achane thalavedana edukkununnaa parayane." ("Don't make such a big noise. Your father says he is getting a headache with all the noise.")

But when the kids played outside, Amma and Velliamma could be seen looking through the bars of the window and chuckling at the chaos before them. All was right, at least for the moment, in their little universe.

CHAPTER 5

T*he parallel college was situated* in the heart of the little town. "College" was an overly ambitious term for the six rooms with a capacity for thirty unhappy souls to a room. The outside desperately needed a coat of paint, but finances were always tight, and it had to wait. When it rained during the Kerala monsoons in the months of June and July, the roof leaked in several places. The students often rearranged the meager furniture of benches and desks to avoid being drenched by a steady stream of water. Several classrooms had buckets. They were part of the furniture, and came in handy when the rains hit the porous roof in a hard pitter patter.

The students were a mixed bag. Most were rejects from the more prestigious institutions due to poor grades. These "branded" ones were glad to be attending any sort of college, although previous failures had not taught them the lesson of perseverance in their academic endeavors. They were generally happy, carefree, and out for a good time while trying to figure out what they wanted to do in the serious world of living.

CHAPTER 5

Then there were people like Lakshmi, who knew they were too good for parallel college, but because of parental bullheadedness (or lack of means), had no choice. In general, these people were an unhappy lot with a chip on their shoulders and prone to bad temper. But to a person, they tried hard to apply themselves in their studies, hoping that redemption would come by being able to join a regular college. Lakshmi was determined to make the most of this situation; she was going to become a teacher somehow. She sat earnestly in the front row, with notebook and pen in hand, flanked by her friends Aarathi, Sumithra, Rajalakshmi, and Divya.

The lecturer was a young man in his mid-thirties with a new master's degree in mathematics from a no-name college. Having no previous teaching experience, he was relegated to working at a parallel college. He was also making the most of the situation while awaiting a better placement in a regular college or at another institution of higher learning.

His glasses solidly framing his small head, he walked in clasping his textbooks, his leather sandals making a soft "thwack, thwack" on the cement floor. "Good morning Vikram Saar (Sir)," the students chanted in unison, rising to their feet. The ones in the back craned their heads to get a good look at this mathematical prodigy.

He directed the class in a nasal voice: "Good morning, good morning, ellaavarum irikku." ("Everyone please sit down.")

He introduced himself and elaborated on his master's degree, the most notable achievement in his life.

He went on, "Ellavarkum textbook kittiyo? Ithe mathene ella collegekalum follow cheyyana syllabus aane." ("Did everyone get their books? This is the same syllabus that is followed by every good college in this state.")

After the introductions, he looked over the class and deigned to smile a little as he asked, "Now, is there anything that you would like to know about me?" He had read that this was how modern professors reached out to their students.

Before anyone could answer, there was a commotion at the door and in trooped a tardy group of three boys. Lakshmi still remembers the first time she set eyes on Hanif Mohamed—his tall, lanky frame, mop of curly hair, and cheeky grin that accentuated beguiling dimples. Nobody remembered that there were two other guys with him, because all eyes were fixed on the confident young fellow. With a dismissive wave of his hand, almost like an afterthought, he said to the teacher, "Sthalam kande pidikkaan korache budhimutti, athonda late aayathe, allengi njaan eppazhum punctual aa!" ("I had a little difficulty finding the place, otherwise I am always punctual!")

In the middle of the little town, the parallel college was the biggest structure. If that were not enough, it was demarcated with a sign that could practically be seen from space, reading, "Parallel College." Hanif Mohamed was the only one who missed that.

There was an audible snicker from the class. The new teacher tried to hide his irritation as he instructed Hanif Mohamed and his two hangers-on to sit on the boy's side of the classroom.

From across Lakshmi's desk, on the male side of the room, the first desk was occupied by Karthikeyan, the most earnest student in the class, who, without fail, answered most of the problems put to them by their teachers. However, the more he ingratiated himself with the teachers, the more unpopular he became with the students. He thought of Lakshmi as a kindred spirit exploring the world of mathematics, and he thought this was a perfect opportunity for him to draw a line of distinction between himself and the likes of Hanif Mohamed.

He said to Lakshmi in a stage whisper, "Scoolile thottathe mathiyaagaande thallippoli ividem etheettinde." ("Not content with failing just about every class in school, the good-for-nothing has appeared here too.") She shook her head in assent, but could not take her eyes off this new Adonis who had descended on their classroom.

With an irritated look in the direction of Hanif Mohamed and his gang, the teacher said, "So, as I asked before, are there any other questions you want to ask me before I start class?"

The cheeky one raised his hand. He dared to ask, "Saaru kalyaanam kazhichittundo?" ("Are you married?") The class burst into laughter.

Vikram Saar looked flustered. With a murderous glance at his tormentor he replied sarcastically, "Illa, ini ente kudumbathe patti vellathum ariyano avo?" ("No, next would you like to know something about my family?") Without waiting for a reply, he started to take attendance. "Karthikeyan?" "Present, Saar." "Lakshmi Shankaran?" "Present, Saar." The day dragged on with no more drama.

At the end of the lesson, Vikram Saar wrote a fresh problem on the blackboard. "If the hypotenuse of a right angled triangle is 6 m long with an incline of 25 degrees, what would be the angle of the other two inclines?" His chalk squealed across the board as if to underline the torture inflicted upon the students.

The class sighed and the teacher put up his hand. "Venda, venda, ippo cheyyaanalla, veetteenne cheythitte vanna mathi.

Naale ithe nammude kanakke vidwaan Hanif Mohammad avatharippikkunnathaayirikkum!" ("No, no this is not for today; you guys can take it home and work it out. And our math whiz, Hanif Mohamed, will take us through the steps of the problem tomorrow.")

Gotcha! The teacher had not forgotten the perceived insult from his young pupil and, petty man that he was, he was getting back at him. For a moment, Hanif Mohamed's handsome face fell, but he recovered quickly. He said, in his usual jaunty way, "Athinenda saare, angane aavatte, njaan padippikkana kemam konde saarinde joli povaandirunna mathi!" ("That's no problem sir, I can manage, my only fear being that because of my great teaching methods, your job might be in danger!")

Vikram Saar's hour of teaching was over. He left the classroom with a malicious look towards his unruly charge. Lakshmi felt for the young man, who meant no harm with his careless remarks. She knew the instructor wanted to teach Hanif Mohamed a lesson by showing him up as a poor student. At lunchtime, when the class emptied out, she quickly worked out the problem and left the paper folded like an envelope on Hanif Mohamed's desk.

All night long she tossed and turned on her hard mattress wondering what had made her do such a daring thing. She hoped that no one had seen her casually leaving the paper at a boy's desk, and, to make matters worse, a Muslim boy! Gossip travels faster than lightening. If her parents heard about it, all hell would break loose and there was no telling what consequences would follow. Despite all this, there was an air of vulnerability to the young man, which was impossible to resist. The next morning, she dressed carefully and could barely eat breakfast before going to school. When she spilled her morning coffee at the dining table, Nalini was irritated. "What is wrong with this girl today? She is all thumbs!"

Reaching school, Lakshmi sat at her usual desk and waited for Vikram Saar to start his class. For a few minutes, she lived in terror that Hanif Mohamed would not show up for fear of being exposed. But she need not have worried. Barely three minutes later, the mischievous grinning face arrived at his usual desk.

Vikram Saar began an elaborate preamble of how he hoped everyone had done the problem and understood the rationale behind the question. Then, like a vulture playing with his prey, he looked towards Hanif Mohamed and sweetly said, "Now I ask Mr. Mohamed to take us through the steps of how he solved the problem." He then sat down on his chair as if yielding the floor to a great master.

Hanif Mohamed went up on the platform, picked up the chalk, and in neat lines proceeded to work out the problem step-by-step, leaving the class gaping. When he was finished, he stepped down from the platform and waited modestly for instructions from the teacher. Disappointment danced like flames on Vikram Saar's face; he curtly ordered Hanif Mohamed to return to his desk.

As the cheeky one walked towards his desk through the center aisle of the classroom, he caught Lakshmi's eye, and she smiled at him.

CHAPTER 6

"*Shhhh, shhhh.*" *Lakshmi thought she heard* someone calling from behind her. She was walking home from college, hugging her textbooks to her chest. When she turned around, he was walking towards her, with the angle of the sun making him look like a visual image of light. The goofy grin was there. Hanif Mohamed was back to his usual self.

He caught up with her, and in his casual way he ventured, "Ente Kazhuthe kolakke kodukkaathirunnathine nanni! Ayaalenne onnu aattaan erangi porapettatha! Thaan enne rakshichu." ("Thanks for saving my neck! He was getting ready to torture me.")

Lakshmi grinned at this acknowledgement; it seemed like high praise coming from someone as nonchalant as him. They both kept glancing around to make sure they were alone. If anyone was coming down the village road, they would make a hasty retreat to their own private paths. A young man and a young woman seen talking together was enough to set tongues wagging. And to add oil to the flame, two adolescents from

CHAPTER 6

opposite sides of the spectrum (a Muslim and a Hindu might as well be from separate worlds) it was downright insurgency, as perceived by the old patriarchy.

He continued, "*Vaappa* (father) wanted me to take math. He said that at least I could keep the accounts in the shop straight. He wants me to join his business. I don't want to be a butcher all my life, but my head is as thick as a plank, and I don't seem to get the hang of math either."

Lakshmi now saw the vulnerability of this young man who presented himself with outward composure bordering on brazenness. "But you did quite fine in class the other day explaining the problem. I think you have never applied yourself. If you do, I think you will do quite well." She knew she sounded like a teacher, but she felt he was being too hard on himself.

"Lakshmide note valare clear aayirunnu, enikke manasilaakkan oru budhimuttum indaayilla. Edekke onnu nottukale thanna mathi, njaan onne shramikkatte" ("Lakshmi, your notes were very clear. I didn't have any difficulty understanding. Could you once in a while give me some of your notes so I can try to understand?")

Lakshmi laughed softly in pleasure and embarrassment, nodded her head, and walked away before she could be seen by anyone along the road.

This was how sometimes papers would appear during lunch break at Hanif Mohamed's desk. In return, Lakshmi was rewarded by the warmth in his eyes as he peaked at her when he thought no one was looking. At the time of *Ramzaan* (Ramadan), she found a small plastic packet at her desk. When she had a moment alone to open it, she found a few pieces of *halwa* (a sticky sweet dessert with almonds) inside it. As she mouthed her thanks, he said it was "Gurudakshina" (an offering to the teacher).

Bit by bit, she started piecing together the story of Hanif Mohamed. His father, Mammukkoya, was a butcher in town. On any ordinary day you could see him behind the carcasses hanging in his shop, dressed in a checkered *lunghi* (dhoti), a dirty wife beater undershirt, and a small towel wrapped around his head. His cleaver seemed like an extension of his hand; he was a rough man. He brooked no nonsense from anyone, and was famous around the neighborhood for getting into fights. Rumor has it that he once hacked an opponent so badly in a fight that he later died, but no one would come forward to report the event. It was a tough neighborhood, and Mammukkoya was a man who lived on the strength of his brawn.

Hanif Mohamed's mother, Subeda, was the beautiful daughter of Suleiman, the greengrocer. She was brought up in a world filled with harmony and affection. Her family did not have much, but their house was a home where she and her two sisters grew up together. Subeda was the oldest and the most beautiful. Her lips were red without a hint of lipstick, her limbs were long and graceful; even the small mole on her upper lip looked like a mark of distinction.

Young Mammukkoya was in love with this angel he saw one day walking towards his shop. She shyly held out a ₹20 note and said, "Umma paranju ore kilo aatterachi venamne. Athikam elle vendaanne paranju." ("My mother told me to get one kilo of mutton. She also said not to put too many bones in the meat.")

Mammukkoya was enthralled. He packed the best mutton in his shop, 1½ kg for her to take home, saying, "Ini vella aavashyam indengi ennode paranja matheetto." ("If you need anything anytime, please let me know.")

He was twelve years older than Subeda, and no one would call him good-looking. But he could be charming, and he exuded

CHAPTER 6

a certain confident machismo that made him the undeniable king of Butcher's Lane.

He was so enamored of Subeda that he sent a broker to her house seeking her hand in marriage. Suleiman was trying to raise a family of three girls with the meager income from selling vegetables for a profit of mere *paisas* (pennies). He looked up to Mammukkoya as a strong leader; someone who could take care of his family well. So Suleiman managed to scrape together ten sovereigns' worth of gold in necklaces and bangles for the wedding.

The new gold glowed brightly on Subeda—she looked like a queen. Mammukkoya was ecstatic; he had married the most beautiful girl in town. He took her to his home. Although modest, it was much larger than what she was used to. Besides, he had added an extra bedroom to one side of the house. He had Raman, the local painter, colour the outside of the house in bright pink to prepare for his bride's arrival. The new bedroom was called "Subeda's room," and it was as if Mammukkoya had built his own version of the Taj Mahal for the love of his life.

At first, everything seemed idyllic for the young couple. Mammukkoya brought home the best tidbits from his shop for his wife to cook kormas and biriyani; they lived in wedded bliss. He no longer got into fights. Even his detractors found him a trifle more benevolent and forgiving. Subeda had that effect on him.

Before long, she whispered to him that she was expecting a baby. He was ecstatic. "It will be a son!" He was sure of it. And soon enough, it was as if the gods had heard him, because Subeda delivered a healthy baby boy.

Little Hanif Mohamed had inherited his mother's good looks, her curly hair and dimples, and her long limbs. Mammukkoya was so proud of his little golden child that the day of his birth, anyone who came to the butcher shop got more meat than they had bargained for—at half prices. He was seen giving out alms to the poor souls begging for a few paisas on the street.

When Subeda left her parents' home after the delivery, upon her arrival at the house they shared, Mammukkoya treated the relatives on both sides of the family with biriyani and *pathiri* (a rice flour pancake). And for dessert there were halwas of all kinds—*badam* (pistachio), cashew, and jaggery.

He paid ₹300 for a rocking cradle for the newborn, which he proudly carried home and established in their bedroom. Little Hanif Mohamed could not have asked for a better entry into this world.

Although at first Subeda seemed happy with her beautiful son and the lavish attentions of her besotted husband, it was soon evident that something was wrong. When Mammukkoya returned home from work, he would find the baby screaming his head off. He soon realized the child was hungry—Subeda had forgotten to nurse him. Her breasts were developing infected abscesses. She lost interest in dressing, and the *athar* (perfume) on her dressing bureau remained untouched.

Sometimes her husband would find her weeping, with the baby in her lap looking up and gurgling at her, unaware of his mother's angst, which we would now call postpartum depression. Subeda's mother, Amina, came to stay with them. She cooked Subeda's favorite foods and tried to jolly her into getting dressed. She even lined her daughter's beautiful eyes with kohl.

For a few days, Mammukkoya felt like he had his old Subeda back, and he was grateful to his mother-in-law. After two weeks, when things had settled down, Subeda's mother returned

CHAPTER 6

home; she still had two unmarried daughters and a husband to look after.

But Subeda's mind continued to play tricks on her. She would alternate between periods of copious weeping and utter joy, when she crooned to her newborn son. It troubled Mammukkoya to see his beloved so unlike her usual placid self—it was as if her mind was raging a war within itself. He worried about her constantly and tried to help with domestic chores. He whisked his little boy from his cradle as soon as he got home.

The neighbors saw the tough man of the street cradling his newborn in the crook of his arm, and walking up and down the veranda singing, "Nee vappaante monalle, ummante karalalle." ("You are your father's son and your mother's heart.") They shook their heads in sadness. Devayani, the kind Hindu lady next door, tried to keep an eye open for the young mother who had lost all heart after the rigors of childbirth.

Even today, Mammukkoya tries to close the door in his heart that threatens to open to memories best kept sealed so that one can go on with life. These are memories of the day he came home from work and found his Subeda hanging from a rope in the storeroom, with its hooks in the ceiling meant to hang heavy bunches of *nendrappazham* (plantains) to ripen. It fell to him to take her body down and lay her on their bed. Mammukkoya's howls of angst reverberated throughout the neighborhood, and people came running.

Mammukkoya stood over his wife's body. "Ennodithe cheyyandaayirunnu Subedo! Njaan ninnodenthe thette cheythittaa? Snehikka maathralle cheythitullo." ("Why did you do this to me Subeda? What wrong did I do? I have loved only you!)

Oblivious, to the tragedy, the baby giggled in his crib. The mother-in-law came and took the baby to her home. From then on, he was fed from a horizontal glass feeding bottle with rubber nipples at both ends.

Mammukkoya showed no interest in his newborn; he felt he had lost everything in life. That is how Hanif Mohamed grew up in his mother's home for the first five years of his life. Vaappa was someone who came with presents at Ramzaan and for his birthday. Hanif Mohamed was a little scared of the burly man with a big mustache; he tried to hide behind his grandmother's dhoti.

When he was five, his father remarried. It was then that Mammukkoya came to take his son to live with him permanently. Not wanting to leave the security of his mother's home, where his grandmother and aunts doted on him, the young boy bawled his head off. But it was his father's wish, and that was the law where Hanif Mohamed was concerned. His stepmother was a kindly enough lady. She always made sure that he was fed, and, when his trousers were too frayed, that he had new clothes made. But soon, her own children were born—first a girl and then a boy.

Indifference crept in, and Hanif, now eight, was left to his own devices. His father rarely interacted with him. He grew up lonely, always with a feeling of being unwanted gnawing at the back of his mind. A mediocre student, he somehow plugged on and reached the level of parallel college, but a scholar, he was definitely not.

Sometimes, young Hanif Mohamed would catch his father looking at him in a peculiar way, and he often wondered whether his father blamed him for the death of his mother. It was a burden no child should have to carry. Although he lived in a house, he felt homeless. This made him reach out to others. He soon found out that he was a welcome addition in his peer group.

CHAPTER 6

Handsome, lively, and charming, he was surrounded by his good friends Bashir, Ravi, Javed, and Saleem. This group went to movies, played cricket in the open fields, and teased girls hurrying to school. Out of necessity, life had found a certain rhythm and cadence, and the enormous portals along the path to adulthood were opened, one by one.

CHAPTER 7

Vikram Saar was most irritated. He said, "Thanikke classil-irikkaan kazhiyillengi athe paranjaa pore, endinaa ellaarem budhimuttikane? Classee varanathe komaali kettanaa?" ("If you don't want to sit in the class, why don't you say that? Why do you want to disturb everyone else? Are you coming to class only to clown around?")

Lakshmi and Hanif Mohamed had completed one year of education at the parallel college. With Lakshmi leaving regular notes of explanation for Hanif Mohamed at their assigned hiding place, he was showing signs of progress in his academic endeavors. There was a natural intelligence about the young man. He grasped things quickly. And since life had taught him lessons he had had to learn on the run, he retained it all in his head with impressive clarity.

When the final exam results in math were tabulated, even Vikram Saar looked surprised as he handed Hanif Mohamed his answer paper. When Lakshmi looked his way, he just lifted the corner of the exam paper where his mark was displayed—it said 80/100! This was a giant leap for the young man whose grades had previously hovered around a barely passing thirty-five points. She smiled and looked away, exulting in a victory shared.

※

Throughout the summer, she had been listless, a feather tossed in the wind. She missed her secret role of teacher extraordinaire. Even the arrival of her cousins for the summer vacation did not fully fill her mind. They no longer played hopscotch as they had in childhood. They sat under the coconut trees talking about movies and colleges and dreams.

She did not tell them that the day after exams, as she walked to the temple to give thanks to the gods as Amma had instructed her, she rounded a quiet bend on the unpaved road and heard the familiar "Shhh, shhh."

When she turned around, there was Hanif Mohamed, holding out a yard's length of Jasmine garland. "Enne ithrem sahaayichathine enikke onnum tharaanilla! ente oru cheriya sandosham" ("You have helped me a lot, and I don't have anything suitable to give you. This is just a small token of my appreciation.")

Lakshmi looked around before she stretched out her hand. In the years that followed, she played this scene over in her mind a thousand times and wished she could have prolonged that short contact. It was a gesture of nobility on the part of two people of different religions who might as well have been separated by a sea, a gesture meant to sustain them for a lifetime.

"Ithinde onnum aavashyam indaayirinnillaatto. Njaan athrem onnum cheythittilla." ("You didn't have to do all this; I have not done that much for you.") But she wove the garland carefully into her long braid. Still flustered and basking in Hanif Mohamed's masculine attention, she smiled and walked away.

❈

When they resumed their studies the next year, true to form, Hanif Mohamed and his buddies walked in late to Vikram Saar's class. This did not improve the teacher's mood.

Lakshmi noticed that he had put on quite a bit of height and his lean body was becoming muscular, probably from working at the butcher shop. He had a two days' worth of growth on his face and although it hid his dimples, it made his face more manly and strong. There was also a certain newfound confidence—he looked like a person in charge of his destiny.

This did not mean that he—along with his willing buddies—was above his usual clowning to make the girls laugh. As Vikram Saar turned to write on the chalkboard, Hanif Mohamed mimicked his stiff gestures and exaggerated speech. Everyone tried hard not to laugh too loudly.

Today was another such day. Hanif Mohamed was in rare form as the class clown. To Vikram Saar's admonishment, the unrepentant student said, "Ayyo Saare, angane parayaruthe, njaanee classine vendiyalle jeevikkanathe." ("Please don't say that sir, you know I live only for this class.") The class grinned behind covered mouths at the impunity of the boy. Vikram Saar gave him a murderous look, then, sighing in resignation, he proceeded with the class.

That afternoon, after lunchbreak, Lakshmi found a small piece of paper with a note written in his terrible handwriting: "Njaan classee varanathe saarine kaanaanonnum allaatto! Veroraale kaanaanaa." ("I'm not coming to this class to see the teacher. I am coming to see someone else.")

CHAPTER 7

The slow blush that started in her cheeks spread to the rest of her face. And in the eyes of the young man who was carefully watching her reaction, she was transformed into the goddess of his dreams. It was a revelation of such proportions that neither knew how to deal with the moment. Although they appeared to avoid each other, they were acutely aware of each other's presence.

Lakshmi put away the note next to the jasmine flowers, which had by then dried up inside her notebook. She tucked them both away in her heart.

CHAPTER 8

M*ammukkoya was in rare form today.* It was a Friday morning, the day his Muslim brethren would be out in force at the mosque for evening prayers. He looked forward to the camaraderie of like-minded worshipers and the bits of gossip they exchanged about trade and social life.

Friday also meant the sale of meat would jump two-fold. Families would come to buy beef, mutton, and chicken. Mammukkoya did brisk business on Fridays. His till rang with the sound of notes and coins being deposited, and he kept this box well hidden from the eyes of his customers and his help. He literally sat on it!

Today he was being the genial merchant, inquiring about the health of the customers' families and making the general small talk that accompanied each purchase. He was telling Menon Saar, the cashier at the bank, "Ithe Mammukkalle parane, nalla aluva polethe erachiyalle, ivide vetteetha, njaan angane ningale chathikko." ("This is Mammukkoya you are talking to; the meat

CHAPTER 8

here is soft like halwa; the animal was slaughtered here. Would I cheat you?")

Menon Saar gave him a ₹50 note and turned to leave. Mammukkoya confronted him. "Athe shariyalla sare, ithe atterachiya, vellia velaya, 60 rupayaanatta." ("That is not right, Menon Saar, this is mutton and it is more expensive. It is ₹60 per kilo.") Menon Saar shook his head in disgust, took a ₹10 note from his pocket, gave it to Mammukkoya, and walked away.

Mammukkoya was brimming with excitement when he greeted his next customer, an old friend. Out of the corner of his eye he had seen Moideenkutty drive up in a brand new Maruthi, the car's bright red finish gleaming in the hot Kerala sun.

"Alla ithaaraa Moideenkuttiaa gulfienne, kanditte manasilaayillaatta, thadiche velutha jubbem itte oru raashtreeyakkaarante pole, nalla stylan caraatta." ("Wow, if it is not old Moideenkutty from the Gulf. I did not recognize you at first, all fattened up and wearing a tunic, I thought you were a politician. Your car looks really stylish.")

Moideenkutty, resplendent in a white *jubba* (tunic) and white dhoti, wearing Ray-Ban sunglasses, and with two or three gold rings on his fingers, looked the picture of prosperity. "Let me have 4 kg of your best mutton, no bones please. My wife is making biryani for the whole clan today. What can I say? How are you doing?"

Mammukkoya feigned modesty and replied, "Njangale paavangalum ingane jeeviche ponu, 4 kilone 240 rupayaavum, kozhappamillallo?" ("We poor people are somehow surviving, four kilos of mutton will cost you ₹240, that's okay with you, right?")

With a dismissive wave of his hand, Moideenkutty gave the okay for the purchase, and Mammukoya got busy making up the big order. He sharpened his long butcher knife and started cutting pieces with a sure hand, each piece cut with almost machine-like precision.

Hanif Mohamed was helping his father with the early rush hour, packing the meat and ringing up customers before he could hurry home, bathe, and get ready for classes at the parallel college. He, too, was impressed with the shiny new Maruthi parked in front of the butcher shop.

While waiting for his meat to be packed, Moideenkutty turned his attention to Hanif Mohamed. "Edaa Hanife, nee vellia cherukkanaayalloda, vellathum padikkanundo, atho ee thozhil thanneyaano plan?" ("Hey Hanif, you have become so tall. Are you studying something, or are you planning to end up in the same profession as your father?")

Hanif Mohamed explained that he was attending the parallel college and studying mathematics. He was pleased to see that old Moideenkutty was more than a little impressed. But Hanif was more interested in hearing about Moideenkutty's life in Dubai.

Moideenkutty was happy to oblige. "Ippo nammade aalkaare nadathane oru canteenile supervisaraa. Tharakkedillaatha shambalom, veedum okke inde, pakshe avade chennethikkittaan korache paade pettu!" he said. ("Right now I am a supervisor in a canteen run by our people. The salary is okay, and I get a small living quarters. But I did struggle a lot to get to this place!")

He went on to tell Hanif Mohamed how he had set sail in a small sailboat from the coast of Chaavakkaad, about twenty miles from where they were, and the perilous journey he had undertaken in the small vessel with its crew of twelve. "There were times I thought I would never see my wife and family again. When the Arabian Sea heaves with all its might, it is a scary

CHAPTER 8

sight for the eyes. I give full thanks to Allah for getting me to the other side safely." His eyes were misty with the memories of his early struggles.

Mammukkoya's raspy voice broke the spell. "First-class mutton ready, thante ummanode para ithe Mammukkoya swandam kayyonde eduthe thannathaanne." ("First-class mutton is ready, you tell your wife that Mammukkoya personally cut this with his own hands for you.")

Moideenkutty handed the butcher payment for the meat. Then, taking out a ₹20 note, he gave it to young Hanif Mohamed with a chuckle. "Go and buy something for yourself, try to study hard and get ahead, this is no job (with a general wave towards the shop) for a young man with dreams." Then he got into his car and drove away with a flourish.

Mammukkoya, while happy enough to get the money, was a little offended at the last remark demeaning his profession. His next customer was Joseph, the barber. Mammukkoya said with irritation, "Ippo avan vellia mothalaaliyalle, njangale kaliyaakkaan, innale vare njaanividathe elle parakki koduthittaa,veetile koottaan indaakeethe!" ("Oh, he's a bigshot now, making fun of us poor people, but I remember the time when I packed up the odd bits and bones from the shop for him to make some semblance of a curry at home!")

But Hanif Mohamed could not get the story of Moideenkutty travelling all the way to Dubai through the waves of the Arabian Sea out of his head. While walking to college with Bashir and Ravi, it was all he could talk about. Bashir tried to dampen his enthusiasm by injecting a note of caution. "Kore pere chathum poyittunde, bhayangara dangerasaa." ("A lot of people have also died trying to do this. It is extremely dangerous.")

CHAPTER 9

I*t was a September afternoon* that would be forever etched in Lakshmi's memory. With one final instruction to the class not to forget what they had learned, Vikram Saar dismissed the class, wishing them all a prosperous Onam.

It was harvest time. For the people of Kerala it was the time to celebrate the abundance of nature. It is a state holiday, one when most institutions, schools, and other establishments are usually closed. People come out in their new clothes and every house prepares the grandest of vegetarian dinners, called *Sadhyas*, which are eaten on banana leaves.

The legend surrounding Onam is even more remarkable. It revolves around the selfless act of the great King Mahabali, who ruled Kerala thousands of years ago, when peace and prosperity prevailed in the land. He was such a great ruler that even the gods were jealous. They conspired to bring him down. In a supreme act of duplicity, they sent him into the underworld. The king's last wish was typical of his greatness: that he be

CHAPTER 9

allowed to visit his people once a year. This coincides with the celebration of Onam.

Lakshmi and her friends had gathered flowers of different colours from around their neighborhood. In front of each house were intricate patterns drawn on the ground and filled in with flowers. Celebration was in the air. In the kitchen, Amma was preparing the snacks for the household and for company. Lakshmi's aunts and their children would stay with them for a couple of days. It was all extremely exciting.

The heady smell of banana chips being fried in coconut oil wafted through the house. Thangam, the part-time maid, was heard grating the coconuts on her *cherava* (a footstool contraption with a serrated metal tongue at the end). For Onam, there were very few curries that did not involve coconuts in some form—ground, grated, puréed, or simply squeezed to extract the coconut milk.

The boys in the classroom, with a general "Happy Onam" in the direction of the girls (again, neither the college nor society encouraged them to mingle freely with the opposite sex), walked out of class, still discussing the latest football (soccer) game they had seen played.

In the sixties, Indian households did not own televisions. People got their news and the results of sporting events through newspapers, radio, or the newsreels played before each movie.

Ravi, the undoubted sportsman of Hanif Mohamed's group, was expounding on the latest state-level football match. "Matte teaminte forward ore headeraa kaachi, pakshe Victor Manjilede ore save alle kaanande!" ("The forward on the other team tried to do a header and score the goal, but you should have seen the save by Victor Manjila, the Kerala goalkeeper!") The others nodded their assent as they filed out of the classroom.

Lakshmi was excitedly chattering to Divya. "Amma Parayanathe ee onathine sariyaakkaamenna, ini daawini praayokke poyeenne." ("Amma keeps saying it is time I started wearing a sari; that I have outgrown my half sari status"). She giggled.

Half sarees are a traditional dress worn in South India by young girls before they attain mature womanhood. At fifteen, Lakshmi and her friends had been at that giddy stage—neither girls nor women. As a concession to this limbo state, they wore a half sari—a full printed skirt with a plain matching sari blouse, and a plain three-yard-long sari (as opposed to the six-yard-long adult sari with pleats in front). In this way, the young girls did not have to bother with the more modest, but cumbersome, front pleats. But now that they were sixteen and seventeen years old, it was time to show them off as young ladies who were suitable brides.

Divya pulled her leg. "Appo endaayirikkum penninte ore deenge," she said. ("I can only imagine how vain you will be when that happens.") They were still going on about this new threshold to womanhood, and the wonderment of it all standing on the other side!

When they reached Divya's house, they said their goodbyes. "Appo holidays kazhinjitte kaanaatto, Happy Onam, puthia sari udithitte studiole poyitte photo idukkanam ketto." ("Okay then, I'll see you after the holidays. Happy Onam! When you wear your new sari for the first time, you should go to the studio and take a photo.") Divya went into her house.

Lakshmi still had a two-mile walk to her house. It was in a more rural part of the small town, and she hastened, acutely aware

CHAPTER 9

of the almost deserted dirt roads with an occasional makeshift shop here and there.

Then, out of nowhere, the heavens opened! Sheets of rain made little rivulets in the soil, and thunder and lightning ripped the sky. Where there had been sunshine a minute before, it was now dark and gloomy. Everyone ran for cover. Because it was the tail end of the monsoon season and the rains had almost drizzled to a stop, few had thought to carry an umbrella.

Lakshmi cursed herself. "Ayyo, ee mazhakke varaan kanda ore samayam, nananje naarum." ("Oh dear, what a time for the rains to come, I will get drenched all over.") She tried to walk as fast as possible to maintain a certain dignity, and to not look foolish like the street urchins, who scatter off like so many mice when the rains come.

"Shhh, shhhh." She heard that familiar sound again. When she looked around, there he was, with an umbrella big enough for two. His eyes danced with mirth at her futile attempts to ward off the rain. Despite herself, Lakshmi had to giggle. He reached her and suddenly they were standing under his umbrella, laughing!

"Thante kayyile kodayonnum illaanne manassillaayi, paavam veruthe nayandaanne vichaarichu." ("I knew you didn't have an umbrella, and I didn't want you to get all wet.") She was touched by his caring, and his nonchalance tickled her.

"Endaa neeyende kaavalkkaaranaa enne rakshikkaan?" ("So, are you my guardian to save me like this?") To which the young man replied with his usual engaging candor, "Angane thannenne vecho! Thanikke virodham onnum illallo." ("Well, if you say so! You don't have any problems with it, do you?")

No. She had no problems with it. In fact, the only thought in the young woman's mind as she stood by his side, inhaling the essence of all that is young and fresh and beautiful, was that this moment should last forever. But just as she was about to say something sassy back, a raspy voice behind her broke the spell of the moment.

"Alla, ithe nammade Shankarande molalle, endaa ee mazhethe nikkane, vegam veettee povaan nokke." ("Why, aren't you Shankaran's daughter? Why are you standing here in the rain? Try to get home quickly.") It was the village marriage broker, Narayankutty, wearing his white dhoti and half-sleeved white shirt that was a little too big for his emaciated figure. He was clutching his signature black book in which he had all the names and details of prospective brides and grooms. He gave Hanif Mohamed a calculating look.

Lakshmi, suddenly nervous, felt she had to explain. "Ithe ende claassile kuttiya, note koduthatha." ("This kid is from my class. I was just giving him one of my notes.") Thrusting one of her notebooks into Hanif Mohamed's hands she said, "Ithe copy cheythitte pinne eppazhengilum thannaa mathi." ("You can copy this note and give it back to me whenever you are finished.")

The broker insisted on taking Lakshmi under his umbrella for the one-and-a-half mile walk to her house. Arriving home, Lakshmi went to change her clothes, and Amma fussed: "Kutty kodayonnum kondovaande mazha nananje pani pidikkaanaa pone." ("The girl didn't take an umbrella and has come back all drenched; she is going to catch a fever.")

Narayankutty asked if her husband was around. When Shankaran came out of the bedroom where he was resting after work, he and the broker sat in the veranda talking in hushed whispers. When Nalini offered them steaming hot glasses of tea, they stopped talking and waited for her to return to the kitchen

CHAPTER 9

before resuming. When he finished his tea, the broker stood up and proclaimed that he had a meeting with a prospective client. With a nod in the direction of Nalini, he made a hasty exit.

While changing her clothes, Lakshmi heard her parents talking in worried tones, and knew there would be trouble. The call came soon enough: "Lakshmee, ingote vanne, ore kaaryam chodikkaanunde." ("Lakshmi, come here, I need to ask you something.") Her father's voice sounded stern.

When Lakshmi came to the veranda her father asked her, "Naaraayankutty paranju neeyaa Muslim chekkande koode kodele ninne varthaanam parayaayirunnunne. Endaa aalkkaarekkonde athum ithum pareppikkano? Avande Ummayalle thoongichatha-the?" ("Naaraayankutty told me you were standing under the same umbrella with that Muslim boy, and that you were talking to each other. Do you want people to gossip about you? Isn't that the boy whose mother committed suicide by hanging?")

Lakshmi was in tears. "I was just giving him a notebook because he is trying to bring his scores up in math. There was nothing more!" she lied.

Her father replied, "Ini vellia varthaanom note kodukkalum onnum venda. Maryaadakke poyi vellathum padikkan nokke. Ammoomma anne paranjathaa penkuttiole padippikkaan vidanathe aapathaanenne." ("You can stop all this nonsense of giving notes and talking. Try to concentrate on your studies. Grandmother had warned that trying to educate girls was dangerous.") Lakshmi's mother nodded her head in agreement.

Frustrated, Lakshmi ran to her room.

CHAPTER 10

Lakshmi walked to school as if she was walking on air! For the first time she was wearing an orange sari with bold black flowers printed all the way across the border. She felt like a new woman, one who knew she looked good. Her heart beat in anticipation, looking for a certain affirmation.

"Pennonne minungeettundallo! Eashwaraa kaanaan Sharade pole inde tto," Divya commented. ("Wow you really are shining today! You look like the movie star Sharada.")

"My father took me to Fashion Fabrics and allowed me to choose my first sari. I could not make my mind up, the selections were so great. But I thought this colour would suit my light brown complexion. When we brought it home, Amma also liked it, which was a great endorsement. Because you know, she never likes anything that I pick."

Divya was excited. "How many did you get?" she asked.

Lakshmi replied nonchalantly, "My mother said I have come of age and should hereafter be seen outside the house only in a

CHAPTER 10

sari. We got four medium-priced sarees to wear to college, and two for special occasions like weddings and the temple festival."

Divya stored this information away as ammunition to pester her parents to let her wear the grown-up sari.

Soon they were caught up in the small flow of humanity going towards their classroom. Lakshmi and Divya took their usual seats side-by-side on the bench and opened their textbooks. A few minutes later, in walked Hanif Mohamed with his jaunty loose-limbed walk. As he surveyed the class, his eyes lingered on a particular girl who was feeling extremely self-conscious. For a moment his eyes registered something unfathomable, and the girl blushed. The next minute the mischievous dimples were back. He sauntered to his bench across the room from Lakshmi. When he neared her desk he whispered under his breath, "Lakshmi teacherekke sukham thanne alle?" ("How are you, Lakshmi teacher?") Although innocuous, the greeting had all the familiarity of a warm touch, and Lakshmi giggled.

Divya was indignant—partly out of jealousy, and partly because of the open affront to the prevailing social norms. "Chekkande vellia oru punnaaram. Aduthe poyaa aade narunnundaavum." ("The silly boy with his flirting. I bet if you go near him you can smell goat on him.") This was a reference to his father's occupation.

But in Lakshmi's mind, it was a moment to be treasured, a confirmation of her womanhood from someone constantly on her mind. She remembered her mother's admonition when she was about to leave for parallel college: "Collegee poyitte padikkaande, vella cherukkanem nokki nadanna, Achan padutham niruthum. Njaan paranjillaanne venda." ("If you are going to college to get interested in some boy, let me warn you. Your father will cut your studies short. Let it not be said that I didn't tell you this!") So Lakshmi controlled the clouds in her head and went back to her books.

✽

Later that day, back home, Lakshmi looked over Balan's math test.

"Endamme inganeyundo oru marathalayan! Amme ivane kanakkile naalpathile pathe maarkaa kitteerikane. Naale questionile moonnum thette. Maramandan." ("Dear God, how can there be such a blockhead! Mom, did you see that he has gotten only ten marks out of forty in math. Of all four questions, he got three of them wrong. Idiot!")

Lakshmi could not understand why Balan found a subject that she truly loved to be so onerous. She tried to teach him, but he was not an easy pupil, being fidgety and lacking any motivation to succeed. It did not help that because he was the boy of the household, the son and heir who would look after them in their old age, his parents indulged him. Amma and Ammoomma always made excuses for him. "Avan aankuttialle, korachokke kusirthi indaavum." ("He is a boy, and it is only natural that he will be a little mischievous.")

This time though, Lakshmi could tell that even Amma was starting to get anxious about her *kuttan's* (darling son's) lack of scholastic aptitude. She was heard muttering in the kitchen as she washed the cut plantains for her aviyal: "Ente Bhagavaane, ithendore vidhi. Penkutti padikkaan midukki, chekkane thalelonnum kerunoollya. Endaa cheyya?" ("Dear God, what kind of fate is this? The girl is so good at her studies, but nothing seems to penetrate the thick skull of my son. What can I do?")

CHAPTER 10

She urged Lakshmi to renew her efforts to make a scholar of Balan. When Amma's back was turned, Lakshmi gave him a good "thwack" on the back of his head before helping him with his math homework. Balan whimpered a bit, but he knew that his mother had reached the end of her rope; this was no time to appeal to her soft spot for him.

So there they sat, the determined teacher and the sullen pupil, until it was time for dinner. The spoilt boy was building up a deep, pernicious resentment that even he was unaware of, as he sullenly tried to take in the intricacies of mathematics. As Lakshmi put Balan through his paces with a determined look on her face, she was oblivious to the dark vibes creeping into her young life.

CHAPTER 11

A *patina enveloped Lakshmi*: Her skin glowed, her eyes shone like bright stars, and she basked in the glory of a certain young man's attention. When she arrived in class, her eyes—without her permission—strayed to the seat across the room. Often, they happened to meet a laughing pair of eyes. This made her look away before her secret could be revealed to the world.

When she saw him waiting before class in the compound with his friends Bashir and Ravi, all of them gesturing frantically as they discussed the latest football scores, she could feel his eyes following her as she walked to the classroom.

Divya was sure this was a one-sided infatuation on the part of the butcher's son. She earnestly warned her friend: "Aa cherukkande vichaaram ninakkavanode premam indenna. Onne kanakke paranje kodukkumbozhekkum athe premam aavillaanne para! Pinne erachi vettukaarande bharya aagaan vellia mohalle." ("That boy thinks that you're in love with him. Just because you are helping him with his math, tell

CHAPTER 11

him there's no more to it than that. As if you are dying to be a butcher's wife!")

Lakshmi was aware of the impossibility of her situation. She and Hanif Mohamed were like two planets that shared the same universe, but were on entirely different trajectories—separated by their differences in religion, culture, and socioeconomic background. Her rational self knew this, but deep within her was a primordial need to connect with something larger and more universal than the mundane worries of everyday life.

Then came the letter that changed the course of her life.

Lakshmi was packing her books after class when she felt the heaviness of her math notebook. As she was about to shut it, she noticed a thick letter tucked away in the center of the notebook. Instinctively protective, she closed the notebook before Divya could notice what was in it.

She walked beside her friend through the winding country roads, pretending interest in the latest movie Divya was recounting in minute detail. Her heart was beating fast as she mulled over every possibility of what the letter might say. She was excited, yet scared. She felt that life was running away, like a car without brakes.

Once or twice, she became aware of Divya's irritated voice calling her back from her reverie. "Nee endaalochichondaa nadakkane? Vazheele care varanade engilum onne nokke. Swapnam kande chaavanda!" ("What are you thinking so much about? At least look out for the cars on the road. Make sure your daydreams don't end up killing you!")

Lakshmi demurred and kept a fast pace. They said goodbye at Divya's house and Lakshmi walked on. When she reached her house, she quickly ran inside. Amma was making her favorite banana fritters, but today that seemed insignificant. She ran to the little side room where a small table next to a narrow bed with a thin mattress was her study desk. With trembling hands, she took out the letter. She was about to open it when Balan came running in, an emissary from her mother telling her to join the family for tea.

She called out, "De varenu, amme." ("I am coming, Mom.")

Lakshmi quickly hid the letter—to be read later—and joined the family in the small dining room. Despite her preoccupation, when she finished her steaming tumbler of tea, she helped herself to a couple of banana fritters. She was then obliged to finish her chores for her mother.

At the well out back she sent the bucket into the water with such force that her mother chided her from the kitchen: "Onne padukke, ingane poyaal kayare vegam pottum!" ("Do it a little slowly, otherwise the rope tied to the bucket is going to break!")

In no time, Lakshmi had all the big vessels filled with water and finished chopping the assortment of vegetables: *kumbalanga* (winter melon), *mathanga* (pumpkin), *kaaya* (raw plantains) and *padavalanga* (snake gourd) that her mother had put out for making *aviyal* (mixed vegetable curry). Then she went to the *ammi* (the traditional grinding stone) under the eaves of the narrow back porch. With renewed energy she ground the grated coconut, shallots, turmeric, and other spices required for the curry into a smooth paste.

She said, "Amme onne poyi kolathile kulichitte varatte" ("Mom, I am going to the pond for a bath.") This was a small, shallow pond a half mile from the house. It was used by several families for bathing and to wash clothes, since few had running water inside their homes.

CHAPTER 11

Sitting on a stone in the twilight as the sun was about to set, Lakshmi carefully removed the letter she had hidden in her blouse, next to her heart. The girl savored every line and phrase imprinted in there, words that would stay with her through many years. She would return to those words again and again when dark clouds gathered and seemed to envelope everything.

As she read the letter, Lakshmi could almost hear him speaking the words to her!

My Dearest Lakshmi . . .

You know I am not one to wax poetic, but something within me is urging me to write this letter, something tells me that I need to tell you the innermost thoughts on my mind. As a child I lived on the fringes of a family, a part of them and yet, separated by a chasm. Whenever Vaappa looks at me, all he can see is the greatest loss of his life—his dearest wife. I know he feels guilty about feeling this way, but it is as if he cannot help himself. Every now and then I catch him looking at me, and I can see the sorrow etched on his face. His wife, my stepmother, tries to do what she can, but she has two young children of her own.

Like all children without a steady anchor, I try to keep on the good side of things, lighthearted banter and escaping into a world of friends, fun, and laughter. The only reason I came to the tutorial college was because I hated working in the butcher shop. Even the smell of it drives me mad; I don't want to end up there like my father.

Besides, Javed, Ravi, and Bashir were going to the parallel college, so I followed suit. As you well know, I am no scholar and never will be, but I am coming to understand that it is still important to get as much education as one can, even if one had to beg for one's tuition fees from Vaappa, who feels it is a waste of time.

But I am so glad I came to the tutorial college. Otherwise, how would a Muslim boy from a poor family ever meet a beautiful Hindu girl who comes to class wearing an orange sari with black flowers? From the first day of class, it was hard not to notice you.

You are so tall and graceful, and you carry yourself with such dignity; I would say with an almost queen-like poise. And above all, I think you are a kind person with a good heart. Who else would go out of their way to help a stupid boy so he does not make a fool of himself in front of the class, and the teacher who has it in for him.

We Muslims never forget people who help us, and we are told in the Koran that we must help those who need our help. As the year went by and classes ended, I had plenty of time on my hands during summer vacation.

Even while working in the butcher shop or playing soccer in the village field with my friends, you were never far from my thoughts. It was then that I realized that unbeknownst even to myself, I had fallen in love with you.

What began as gratitude towards a fellow student blossomed into something deeper, and infinitely more pure. You have no idea how many times I have waited in the dense foliage near the temple to get a glimpse of you coming to worship—your long hair cascading down your back, adorned with jasmine flowers.

As I saw you immersed in worship, hands joined together, I prayed that somewhere in that beautiful heart, I too had a

CHAPTER 11

place. You are so difficult to read, always composed, and I have often found it hard to fathom in your dignity whether you harbored any feelings towards me, other than those borne out of pity and kindness.

Your friend Divya certainly makes her feelings about me clear whenever she gets a chance. But you are not like her, and in the few times when we have had a chance to interact, I felt that you liked me too. You deserve so much better than what I have to offer now. But I have also given it some thought, and I have formulated a plan as to how I can provide for you in the way you deserve to be looked after.

This plan is still in the early stages, so, my dearest Lakshmi, when you stand before your Gods and ask for their blessings, please tell them to remember a hapless young man who is trying hard. We are both young and I have such strong feelings for you that I am prepared to wait until the ends of the earth for the day we will be together, not worried about what people think or how we are going to live.

I have never written anything so long in my life, and even I am amazed by it, but I will always love you, no matter what, even if you do not share the same sentiments towards me. And in my heart, whether we are together or follow different paths, you will always have my sincerest wishes, and above all, my heart.

Hanif Mohamed

The girl hugged the letter to her chest; it opened a thousand hidden doors inside of her. In the background lurked fears threatening to loom large, and yet, all she could think off was the overwhelming emotions the letter had stirred within her.

There comes a point in everyone's life when yesterday ceases to exist, and tomorrow seems a million miles away; where reality fades under an all-consuming onslaught of raw emotions—the very seed of existence that has driven humankind through the centuries.

After her bath, Lakshmi carefully folded the letter and tucked it back into her blouse. With the setting sun behind her, as she walked towards her house, she looked like a glowing goddess. At home, her mother welcomed her with her characteristic scolding: "Neram ethra aayi poyitte, onne vegam kuliche vannoode! Njaan Balane paranje vidaan thodangeethaa." ("Why did you take so long, couldn't you have finished your bath sooner? I was getting ready to send Balan out to look for you.")

Lakshmi muttered that she had met the lady from next door who had also come to bathe, and while chatting, forgot about the time. This seemed to satisfy her mother, who went to the kitchen as Lakshmi entered her bedroom.

She gently took the letter from her blouse and placed it under her pillow. In the privacy of the night, she could read it over and over, savoring each word and phrase, as if the writer was beside her in person, uttering each endearment from the handsome face whose every line was carved in her heart.

CHAPTER 12

N*alini called to her son* from the washing stone: "Edaa Baalaa, checheede muriyile bedsheetum pillow casum ingotte konde vanne! Onne kazhugi idatte, Ammoomma varumbo kedakkaanullathaa." ("Hey Balan, bring the bedsheet and pillowcase from your sister's bed to be washed. Your grandmother is coming, and she will be sleeping on that bed.")

After the aging great-grandparents had passed away, life was getting back to normal when Nalini's father started having excruciating stomach pains. The local Ayurvedic doctor prescribed some herbal remedies, and a strict adherence to a recommended diet. It did not help much; he started losing a lot of weight. Soon, it was too late. The cancer had spread all over. He did not last very long. After he passed away, the grandmother was left in the family house alone, because her son worked in another town. She started to spend a great deal of time in her children's households. For those who lived in big joint families, the greatest sadness is when the joint family members disappear and they are left alone.

The coarse cement structure built to beat the dirt out of clothes was surrounded by a half-foot cement enclosure with an opening for the water to drain towards the jackfruit tree. Amma was drawing water from the well to do the laundry.

Besides her parents, Lakshmi had the only other bed in the house. Balan slept on a pallet on the floor in the living room. Lakshmi was required to vacate it whenever company came and lie on a *paaya* (mat) on the floor of the bedroom.

Balan was excited at Ammoomma's arrival. Although his parents were extremely indulgent of him, his grandmother carried this indulgence to a new level. She would always give him a little pocket money and make him special tidbits that he loved. At nighttime, when the fireflies flickered in the dark garden, Ammoomma would sit with her legs stretched out, leaning against the pillars of the veranda. These were the times her grandson looked forward to the most. She had many stories from the Mahabharata and the Ramayana in her repertoire. History came to life when she described the famous battle between Rama, the righteous king, and Ravana, the villain king who had abducted Rama's wife, Sita.

Ammoomma told almost as many stories of ghosts—people who met untimely deaths, and whose souls could not attain peace. In the dim light of the veranda, with darkness all around in the garden, Balan found it exhilarating and creepy to listen to the stories, told in his grandmother's raspy voice.

Sometimes his mother would scold him from inside the house: "Baala, Ammoommede kathem kettirikkaande poyikkedanne orangaan nokke. Naale claasollathaa." ("Balan, go and try to get some sleep instead of sitting and listening to your grandmother's stories. You need to go to school tomorrow.")

At these times, Ammoomma would intercede for him, keeping his mother at bay. "Ithum kuttyole padikkandathokke thanyaa. Raamaayanom Mahabhaaratom onnum illyaande ende padithaa?" ("These are all things that kids need to study also. Without learning about the Ramayanam and the Mahabharatam [Sanskrit epics], what education is there?")

Amma would mutter to herself that the old lady was spoiling Balan. But she would go to bed, leaving the two conspirators to carry on with their tales.

※

The morning of Ammoomma's arrival, Lakshmi left early for class at parallel college. Balan had finished his breakfast of *poote* (steamed rice flour and grated coconut in the shape of a cylinder) with *kadala* (bengal gram made into a curry) and was getting ready for school, which began at 9:30 a.m. He gazed into the mirror and admired the little bird's nest he had managed to shape his forelock into. He was satisfied that he did look a bit like his hero, Jayan, from the movies.

After Amma had put away the breakfast things and Achan (father) went off to work with his packed lunch (rice made in the morning and fish curry from the night before), she started her next chore, laundry. She wanted it out of the way and hanging on the lines to dry before it got too hot to work outside.

"Baalaa, aa sheetonne vegam konduvaa, enthore veyilaa, ennitte schoolee pogaan nokke," his mother instructed. ("Balan, please bring the sheets quickly, the sun is so hot out here. And hurry and go to school after that.")

As Balan took up the pillowcase to strip it, his eyes fell upon the folded sheets of paper. His eager hands clawed at them as if they were prey, and his eyes grew wide as he skimmed the letter's contents. Although the grown-ups in the house had been unaware of a little boy listening behind a door, Balan had been privy to all the commotion caused on that rainy day when Lakshmi was escorted home by the marriage broker.

Balan had surmised that she was in trouble for romantic dalliances. Now he knew it was with a Muslim boy—the butcher's son, no less! This was his chance to get even for every time Lakshmi had called him a blockhead because he was slow in math, or had shared his humiliating grades with their parents under the guise of setting him straight.

He forgot about the laundry. Waving the evidence in front of him, Balan ran into the backyard where his mother stood irritated, shielding her face from the blazing sun with her hand.

"Amme, ithe checheede thalonede adeenne kitteedaa. Aa cherukkande ezhuthaa!" ("Mom, see what I found under my sister's pillow. It is a letter from that boy!")

Nalini forgot the sun as she reached out to take the letter from Balan, who was trembling with excitement at his discovery.

CHAPTER 13

*L*akshmi *had dressed carefully that morning.* She wore the orange sari bordered with black flowers that had captivated a young man's imagination. She lined her eyes with kohl to make them look bigger and more sultry, and finished her dressing with an orange dot on her forehead. Her long hair fanned out, a knot at the end of it, down to her backside.

Satisfied that she looked her best, she entered the dining room. Amma was laying out breakfast on the table and although the pootte and kadala looked inviting, she could hardly keep it down for the excitement within herself.

Amma said, "Vellathum kazhikkoo kutty, ee penpillere ellavarum slim beauty aavaan nokkaane.Veettile pani edukkaan nalla aarogyam venam." ("Try to eat something girl, all the young girls these days are trying to be slim beauties. You need a good amount of energy to get the household chores done.")

Amma seemed to be making excuses for her own generous figure. "Amme Njaan pone, collegile late aavum." ("Mom, I am leaving for college right now or I'll be late.")

As each step brought Lakshmi closer to the building of higher learning, her heart beat faster. Uncharacteristically, Hanif Mohamed was already at his bench, as if he, too, was consumed by the anticipation of a reply. She passed by his desk, and with a shy smile, almost as if to herself, she muttered, "Vellya ezhuthu-kaaranaanalle!" ("I believe you are a great writer!")

He heard it, and the charming grin was back on his face. That was all the affirmation they needed. For them, the rest of the day went by in a daze. When afternoon came and classes were dismissed, they were both surrounded by their respective friends and there was no chance of privacy.

But just as Lakshmi, Divya, Arathi, Sumithra, and Rajalakshmi passed by Hanif Mohamed and his friends, he jokingly tossed out to her: "Lakshmi teachere njaan chothicha math problathinte utharam onne tharanam, ennale enikke shariyaayitte padikkaan pattulloo." ("Lakshmi teacher, you must give me an answer to the math problem I had put to you. Only then will I be able to study properly.")

Lakshmi and her friends giggled at the obvious flirtation. Hanif Mohamed's friends slapped him on his back, teasing, "Oru vellya, kanakkapilla. Ennum vattabhoojyaa!" ("A great math genius! You always get a big zero.")

Only the two parties involved knew the depth of feelings and emotions that were exchanged in those casual bantering words.

As Lakshmi stepped into the courtyard of her little house, her smile became more tentative. It was as if she sensed the dark clouds looming ahead. Her father was already back from

CHAPTER 13

work, which was unusual for him. He was pacing the veranda like a caged tiger. Amma and Ammoomma were sitting on the parapet. Amma's hand was supporting her forehead, as if the heavy burden she carried in her head was too much for her neck to support.

Lakshmi put on a cheerful face. Looking towards her grandmother, she asked as she climbed onto the veranda, "Ammoomma eppo vannoo? Maamanaano konduvannathe? Enne kaanaande maaman poyo?" ("When did you come, Grandma? Did uncle bring you here? He already left without seeing me?")

With her hurried volley of questions, the girl was bracing for the inevitable.

"Tchchch!"

Lakshmi reeled back and held her stinging face, which her father had forcefully slapped.

He said, "Nee collegee ponathe kanda chekkammaarude ezhuthe vaangikaanaa? Padikaanenne paranjitte vittadaa, ippo veedine muzhuvan ekkappere varutheelle." ("Are you going to college to receive letters from boys? You said you were going to study, and now look at the bad name you have brought upon our house.")

Shankaran's white-hot temper would not be calmed; he was blaming himself for giving in to his daughter's desire to continue her studies. He muttered to himself in frustration, "Anne njaan paranjathaa collegilonnum povaande maryaathakke kettiche koduthaa madeenne, appo ninakkaayirunnille vellia nirbhandam avale padikkattenne, ippo ellaavarkum samaadhaanam aayille." ("Even at the beginning, I had told everyone that it was better not to send her to college and instead to marry her off, but you were adamant that if she wanted to study that she should be allowed to do so. Now look at the state of things; you must all be very happy now.")

With no one else to blame, he blamed Nalini for having persuaded him to send Lakshmi to the parallel college. She felt the sting of his bitter words.

She said to Lakshmi, "Endinaa kutty ee panikkokke poye, maryaadakke padiche paassaayaa mathiyaayirunnille, ippo kuttam muzhuvan ende thalelaayi. Avale thalli konnitte ippo ore gunom kittaan ponilla." ("Why did you do this, my child? Why couldn't you just study and pass the exams like everyone else? Now the whole blame for your behavior has come upon my head.") Looking towards her husband she added: "And there is no need to beat her to death."

Amma pulled Lakshmi away so Shankaran could not hit her again. Ammoomma looked sad. When Lakshmi started to sob, the women put their arms around her, shielding her from the world.

Lakshmi said defensively, "Njaan aarkkum ezhuthonnum koduthittilla." ("I have not given anybody any love letters.") Although in truth, she had been meaning to write a reply when she had a moment of privacy.

Ammoomma could not comprehend the situation. "Ore chekkande ezhuthe vaangikkiye, endaa parayane, athum ore jonon chekkande, ende eeswaraa, endokke kekkanam!" ("I can't believe you accepted a letter from a boy and that too, a Muslim boy. Dear Gods, what else am I going to hear!")

Shankaran was not to be pacified. He spoke the words that turned Lakshmi's universe upside down. He said, "Padichathokke mathi. Ini nee college ponda. Naattukaare ariyanene mumbe aa brokare viliche, vegam kalyaanam nadathunnathaa ini budhi. Ee veetteenne porathe poyaa njaan kale thalli odikkum!" ("That is enough of studying. There is no need for you to go to college anymore. Before the whole town comes to hear about it, it is better to call the broker and marry her off. You better not set foot outside this house, or I will break your legs!")

Lakshmi pleaded with her father; she promised never again to take even a single letter from the boy. In her desperation, she flung herself at his feet and begged him to let her continue her education.

But Shankaran had resolved to settle the matter in the most efficient way. He took it as a matter of injured personal pride that his authority as the head of the household to make life-altering decisions for the rest of the family had been challenged.

Lakshmi knew she could not change his mind. She retreated to a corner of her room in defeat. Sitting on the floor with her knees pulled up to her chest, the heavy burden of her head rested on her knees. When Amma and Ammoomma tried to coax her to eat some dinner, she did not budge.

Later that night, when Ammoomma came to Lakshmi's room to sleep on the cot, she tried to reason with her granddaughter. "Saarallya kutty, kazhinjathokke ange marannekke, ini bhartaavum, kuttyolum okke aavumbe ithokke nissaaraavum." ("Don't worry my child, just try to forget all that happened. When a husband and children come along, all this will seem insignificant.") She thought these words would comfort her weeping grandchild. But they only brought on a fresh set of tears.

The old woman lay on her bed sighing in defeat at all the things she could not control, even in her little universe. In her helplessness, Ammoomma muttered, "Mulle elele veenaalum, ela mullile veenaalum elakke thanne dosham." ("Whether the thorn falls on the leaf, or the leaf falls on the thorn, it is the leaf that gets hurt.") This was Ammoomma's age-old wisdom regarding the vulnerability of a woman's existence.

Lakshmi's despair was such that even her tears seemed to have dried up. All through the night she sat vigil beside the ashes of her broken dreams.

In the bedroom adjoining Lakshmi's, her father paced restlessly: back-and-forth, covering the small ten-by-twelve-foot room in a few strides. Nalini sat on the bed, agitation rising within her like a storm.

Shankaran had not planned for Lakshmi to be married for a couple of years; he had hoped that some of his *chitti* funds (high rate interest deposits that private companies entice people with) would mature, and that he could use the proceeds to fulfill the parental obligation of marrying off a daughter. But with the unexpected turn of events, that option was unavailable. He went over in his mind how he could come up with enough money to arrange the marriage.

Nalini wrung her hands in helplessness and spoke her fears aloud: "Ini endaa cheyya, kuttiye veruthe veettee nirthiyaale naattekaare muzhuvan ariyum. Pinne kutty vella vidyatharom kaanichaale athe mathi. Ende eeshwaraa." ("What do we do now? If we let her stay in the house in this state, people will start talking. Besides, she might do something stupid. Dear gods!")

Nalini worried that Lakshmi would get in touch with the boy and elope, or, in desperation, commit suicide. While her mother was preoccupied with these issues, her father was trying to figure out a financial way out of the situation.

"Nammade veedinte poragile pathe cente sthalam vitta-ale ore 40,000 roopa kittum. Ore 25 sreedhanathinum, 10 aabharanathinum,athe kazhinje ore 5 kalyaana chelavinum.

CHAPTER 13   79

Angane cheyyaam." ("You know the property behind our house. If we sell ten cents [one hundredth of an acre] of that land, we can get about ₹40,000. Of which ₹25,000 can be spent on the dowry, ₹10,000 on ornaments and there will still be ₹5000 left to conduct the marriage function itself. I think we will do it this way.")

Shankaran was talking about the small piece of land he had bought behind his rental house in hopes of one day building a permanent home for the family. His father had left him a small twenty cents of land, which he had sold, and bought the current property with the proceeds.

Shankaran had made his decision and was satisfied with it. As he sat on the bed and took off his sandals prior to sleep, he told his wife, "Naale jolikke pona vazheele aa chaaya kadele onne ethiche nokkanam. Aa brokere Narayankutty avide irikkindaavum, iniathe businessum nokki. Onningotte vaigunneram ende joli kazhinje varaan parayaam." ("Tomorrow on my way to work, I will go by the tea shop. That broker Narayankutty will be sitting there, soliciting business. I will ask him to come home in the evening when I come back from work.")

Nalini sighed and turned over to the other side of the bed.

The sun rose over the horizon as it does all mornings, unaware of the angst of human beings. All things seemed a little better, careworn people seemed a bit more cheerful, and hope springs eternal in the minds of humankind.

But for Lakshmi, morning found her drained of all emotion. She fell asleep in the early hours in the corner of the room that was her retreat from the world. Ammoomma and Amma woke up and began the morning chores. In a sympathetic unspoken reaction, they agreed to let the girl sleep and hoped a certain healing would begin. It was the realization that all lesser human beings must come to terms with, the limitations of one's own situation.

Shankaran sat stone-faced at breakfast in the dining room, dealing with all the problems that had arisen from the scene on the veranda the night before. His wife and mother-in-law knew better than to try to engage him in casual conversation. They kept to themselves, efficiently moving in and out of the small kitchen serving dosa and chutney and bringing him steaming cups of coffee.

Shankaran washed his hands after breakfast, took up his bag, and carefully placed the lunchbox his wife had prepared into it. He was out of the door in a hurry, a man on a mission. As he left, he called out for Nalini to close the door behind him.

Hearing the voices from the dining room, Lakshmi awoke from a restless sleep. Her limbs ached and her face felt sore. More than that, a heaviness enveloped her heart. It felt as if, overnight, she had added several decades to her spirit. The extreme weariness would not leave her.

Half an hour later, she heard Divya at the veranda calling for her. Amma opened the door and told the other girl curtly, "Ini Lakshmi collegee varinilya. Paditham nirthi. Achan parayane kalyaanam kazhiche kodukkaamenna." ("Lakshmi will not be coming to college anymore. We have stopped her studies. Her father wants to marry her off.")

Lakshmi could almost see Divya's jaw drop, but she did not hear the other girl reply. The warning in her mother's voice must have put off any questions from her friend. Lakshmi started sobbing for herself, for her friend, and for the terrible situation she found herself in.

Then she heard someone whisper her name at the window near the corner where she sat. "Lakshmi, Lakshmi!" She heard it again. She looked out the window to see Divya, who realized that something was terribly wrong. "Ninne kaanaandaayappo enthaa pattie enne nokkaan vannathaa.Inne test olla kaaryam marannoonne vicharichu." ("When I didn't see you coming, I wondered what happened to you. I thought that maybe you forgot about the test today.") She wanted to see if there was some way she could help her dear friend. "Ende patti? Ini collegee varilyaanne paranju. Endaa indaaye?" ("What happened? Why are you not coming to college anymore? What exactly happened?")

In hushed whispers interrupted by sobs, Lakshmi told Divya what had occurred. As she comforted her friend, Divya was overcome with white-hot fury at the injustice of it all. "Aa thendi chekkan cheytha kuttathine, nee endine sahikkanam? Njaan onne chodikkande!" ("Why should you have to pay the price for a crime that was committed by that stupid, worthless boy? I certainly am going to ask him!")

Her friend's reply was even more baffling to Divya. "Athine avan ithra thette endaa cheythe,ithe vellya criminal case onnum allalo." ("So what did he do that was so wrong? This is not a criminal case or anything.")

But Divya was so distraught that she marched straight to college. As she neared the entrance, sure enough, there was Hanif Mohamed standing with Bashir and Ravi. They were arguing about soccer scores.

He said to Divya, "Inne ottakkaanallo, koottine arem kitteele?" ("You seem to be alone today. Didn't you find anybody to walk with you?") This was a subtle inquiry about Lakshmi, whom he missed.

That was all the spark that was needed to light the pent-up fury of Divya's fire. She spat out the words, "Iippo samaadhaanaayille. Avalde padippe nirthi. Ini collegee varillya. Manasaakshiyodonne chodiche nokke aaraa kaaranakkaranenne" ("Are you happy now? They have stopped her education. She will not be coming to college anymore. Ask your conscience who is responsible for it.")

She had the satisfaction of seeing Hanif Mohamed reel at her revelation; he looked stricken. Both Bashir and Ravi were perplexed at the turn of the conversation. They kept looking from one to the other.

Like an avenging angel, the very picture of hell's fury, Divya stomped off to the classroom. Even before his friends could mouth all the questions forming in their minds, Hanif Mohamed took off, without a word of explanation.

That was the last they saw of him for many years. He never returned to college.

CHAPTER 14

A *few days later, the broker Narayankutty* showed up at the door with his characteristic black umbrella and the infamous black notebook with the names of all the hapless men and women his schemes had united (happily—or unhappily) in marriage.

He and Shankaran sat down in the small veranda. Nalini posted herself to the side of the open door to the inside of the house, where she would be privy to their conversation. But her husband instructed, "Nalini nee poyi Narayankuttykke chaaya edukke." ("Nalini, go and get some tea for Narayankutty.")

On the veranda, the negotiations carried on. Shankaran said, "Irupathianchinte sreedhanom, pathinte aabharanom enna vicharikkane, korache budhimuttundaavum, pakshe oppikkaam, sthalam vittittaayaalum." (I was thinking of giving 25,000 rupees in dowry and 10,000 rupees worth of ornaments, it will be a little difficult, but I will try to get it together even if I have to sell some land.)

Naranyankutty looked worried. He muttered, "Innathe kaalathe 25 onnum alla, pennine chowaa dosham alle, athine pattiya aale kandu pidikkande, vellya eluppam olla kaaryam onnum alla." ("Twenty-five-thousand rupees today is not a big sum. Besides, your daughter has the added astrological defect of Chowwadosham. I must find a suitable alliance to go with this Mars-ruled planet, and it is not an easy task.") Of course, he did not add that his brokerage fee was a percentage of the dowry, hence it was also in his interest to increase the sum of the dowry.

By now, Nalini had finished making the tea—with extra milk and sugar to pacify the broker. She called out to her daughter, "Lakshmi nee ithonne kondupoyi koduthe." ("Lakshmi, take this tea to the veranda.")

Lakshmi bristled. "Amma thanne angote kondoyaa mathi, enikkonnum pattilla." ("Why don't you take it yourself, I don't want to.")

Nalini was in no mood for tantrums. She thrust the glasses of tea into Lakshmi's hands. "Vellya varthanam onnum parayandaa. Ella kuruthakedum indaakkeette." ("I don't want to hear any big talk from you. You have created enough problems already.")

Lakshmi carried the tea in a sulk. The broker looked her up and down as she came in. "Kutteede perentha?" ("What's your name?"). He opened his notebook to write it down. Before she could say anything, her father replied, "Lakshmi, vayasse, pathinezhe." ("Her name is Lakshmi, and she is seventeen years old.") He looked at the broker, who was hurriedly taking down the particulars. "If you have nothing else to ask her, maybe she can go into the house now."

Lakshmi went back into the house at this dismissal. It is accepted wisdom in arranged marriage circles that the more exposed the bride is, the more she will be subjected to the critical eye of everyone who can leisurely evaluate her. It was advisable to show a bride in the best possible light for as little time as possible.

Narayankutty made the difficulties of his job clear. "She is a little on the tall side, and her complexion is dusky. Everyone is looking for fair girls. But let me look around and see what I can come up with. My track record is an open book. I have yet to fail in arranging a marriage. I consider this a sacred profession, and I will do everything in my power to find your daughter a suitable boy."

The broker left, having recorded all the salient points of Lakshmi's life in his little notebook. As he climbed down the steps from the house, Shankaran reminded him, "Onne vegam ore kaaryam konde varanam ketto. Athikam samayam kalayandaa." ("Please bring a proposal quickly. There is not a lot of time to waste.")

Narayankutty knew the urgency; he had also heard some rumors, but that was a matter on which the least said the better.

Lakshmi couldn't sleep at night. Her thoughts were hurricanes in her mind. Waves of despair crashed on the rocks of her existence. There would never be a Lakshmi teacher; her dreams of a college degree seemed as rooted in reality as the dreams of a beggar wishing to win the lottery. Like the pendulum of a clock, her moods swung from anger and resentment to depression and resignation.

She felt a burning anger towards her parents and Balan for the helplessness that seemed like the hallmark of her existence.

When her mother insisted that she teach Balan, who could never be accused of being bright, Lakshmi took it out on him. When he had trouble with a math problem, instead of being the patient and sometimes bossy older sister she had been before, now she would give him a few swipes on the head with his book exclaiming, "Marathalayan, ethe janmaano kitteerikkanathe, oru kundom mansilaavinilla!" ("Blockhead, I have no idea what star he was born under, he does not understand a thing!")

One day, during a particularly vitriolic study session, Nalini heard Balan protesting loudly from the bedroom where Lakshmi was coaching him. She marched into the room and confronted Lakshmi. "Logathinodolla deshyam muzhuvan avande thale veche pottichittendaa kaaryam?" ("What is the point of taking out your anger at the world on the head of your little brother?")

That afternoon, when, as was usual now, Divya stopped under Lakshmi's bedroom window after her classes, she found her friend crying in utter despair. She had known Lakshmi since they played hopscotch in the front garden, and it broke her heart to see her friend so helpless. Divya came up with an idea. "Nee karayaandirikke, njaan padiche kazhiyana pusthakam ninakke kondu vanne tharaam. Manasse veruthe punnaaganda." ("Please, don't cry. I will bring you the books that I am done with. That way, you will not lose your mind.")

By way of village gossip, she told Lakshmi that Hanif Mohamed had not returned to class after she confronted him. "Onninum kollaatha chekkan naade vitte kallathoni keri Gulfee poyekkaanennaa ellaarum parene. Kadalee veene chathaa mathiyaayirunnu!" ("Everyone is saying that Hanif Mohamed boarded a small smuggler's boat going to the Gulf. I hope he falls overboard and dies in the Arabian Sea!")

As Divya started to walk away, she was taken aback and felt a little betrayed as she heard Lakshmi say, "He did nothing wrong. How can you wish such terrible things on people? If I am in these straits, it is more a testimony of how narrow-minded my parents and this whole village is. I hope at least he escapes from this stupid place."

Lakshmi wished only the best for the young man with the curly hair and the cute dimples, who showed remarkable courage to cross the boundaries of religion and society and speak from the heart. He was as much a victim of the norms of society as she was, and he, too, paid a price.

CHAPTER 15

As *Hanif Mohamed and nine others sat* huddled on the tarpaulin of a little boat with sails that seemed to hang on toothpicks, the events of the past few days came back to him.

He felt no remorse for having such strong feelings for Lakshmi, but he had a world of regrets for the way it had affected her life, in ways neither of them could have foreseen. He carried a heavy burden of guilt in his heart that she, a promising student, had to forgo her education because of his reckless actions. He saw her in his mind, crying in despair at her dreams being shattered. He would never forgive himself. In his heart he begged her forgiveness a thousand times over. He longed to see her face light up when she saw him.

All that seemed like a fantasy now. In front of him was the unending ocean and a reckless passage to a new world with a tenuous dream of successfully starting over. The masts made a shuddering sound. He looked at the desperate men squatting in the boat, all with their own dreams of leaving behind the

CHAPTER 15

baggage of their unhappy pasts and finding hope and riches in the kingdoms of Aladdin.

Suleiman, the experienced human trafficker, smuggler of gold, and owner of the *dhow* (small sailboat) reassured his ragtag wards. "Athe pedikkaanonnum illaanne, aa paaya onne cherichaa mathi, kaattinde ozhukke maariyathaa." ("There is no need to be scared. We just need to adjust the sails a bit because the wind direction has changed.") Two miles out to sea, the smuggler's boat hugged the coastlines of the countries it passed on the way to the Gulf.

As Hanif Mohamed stared at the sea, he tried to picture the face of his *Umma* (mother), whom he had never seen. It was to this image he prayed. He asked for her forgiveness; he felt he had severed the last tie that bound him to her. He felt an aching emptiness. On the day Divya confronted him about ruining Lakshmi's life, in his despair, Hanif Mohamed had turned around and run.

He sat on the Rocky Hill close to the temple wondering what he was going to do. There seemed to be no future in this small town for him; he did not want to end up like his father, the town butcher.

While Mammukkoya was a rough man, he was strong and streetwise. The boy had inherited his mother's delicate looks and, like her, he had no taste for the violence or the roughhousing and occasional Hindu/Muslim clashes that were frequent in their neighborhood. But he had a strong sense of purpose and determination, and his heart was valiant.

As he sat on that rock trying to salvage his lonely life, he fingered the only material connection he had with his dead mother—the four-sovereign gold chain he always wore around his neck. It had been his mother's chain, and it made him feel close to her.

College was not for him; the only reason he had survived this long was his connection to Lakshmi and her endless help to get him through the exams. It was her face, so poised, and her body, so long-limbed and graceful that she seemed to glide into a room, that kept Hanif Mohamed coming back to class every day. He was captivated.

With that hope gone, he did not want to return to college. When his father heard how his son had left school, Hanif Mohamed knew he would be pressured to work in the butcher shop, and he wanted no part of it. There was only one way out.

He marched straight to one of the town's great institutions, the last refuge of the desperate masses: "Chetty and Sons Swarnam Pandam Panayam Vyaapaaram." (Chetty and Sons Gold Merchants, Pawn Shop.)

Mr. Chetty, proud owner of this esteemed establishment, sat behind the counter at the entrance, his hair slicked back with enough Brylcreem to lubricate a small motorcar, his fingers laden with gold and diamond rings. He was given to grand gestures with his hands; he felt it showed off his rings to advantage.

Hanif tentatively approached him. He carefully took out the heavy chain his Umma wore until the day she died and laid it on the counter. Wordlessly, Chetty's fat fingers assessed the chain; he rubbed it against a stone to determine the purity of the gold. "Swarnam moshallya, ethra indenne nokkatte." ("The quality of gold seems decent enough. Let me see how much it weighs.")

He placed the chain on his little brass weighing scale inside a glass case. Chetty was notorious for never admitting even when the finest quality of gold was brought in. And his weighing scales, according to rumor, had *kuttichaathan* (the devil), sitting in one of them, making sure the item the customer wanted to pawn always weighed less.

The king of pawn looked at Hanif Mohamed. Without batting an eyelash he said, "Ethaande moonnara varum. Pinne namakke baakiollore pattichittendaa kaaryam." ("It weighs about three-and-a-half sovereigns. What do I have to gain by cheating others?")

This was the understatement of the day. The youth argued, to no avail, that the chain contained four sovereigns' worth of gold. He then tried to appeal to Chetty's heart: he said he needed the money to pay his parallel college fees. It was like talking to a brick wall.

Chetty had made up his mind. He made his final offer: "Moonnara pavane ore aaraayiram rupika tharaam. Athe thanne kooduthalaa!" (For three-and-a-half sovereigns, I can give you ₹6000, which itself is too much!") His corpulent body jiggled as he laughed at his joke.

Hanif Mohamed knew he had no bargaining power, and accepted the deal with resignation. As the youth left the store with ₹6000 in his pocket, Chetty called out after him: "Ini thande Vaappa, aa erachi vettana katheem pidiche ende poragi varillaanne orappe parayanam." ("You need to give me assurance that your father will not come after me with his butcher knife that he uses at the shop.")

Even the mighty Chetty feared the wrath of the butcher, who eagerly brandished his knife like a sword and took on anyone who crossed him in the markets.

✹

With time stretching before them like an elastic band, the dhow's passengers spent their time doing the daily chores of living. The ₹3000 each had shelled out for the privilege of this ocean voyage did not purchase five-star accommodations. At the bow of the boat, Suleiman's second-in-command, Abisullah, boiled rice for *kanji* (soupy rice porridge). It was dished out, along with pickled *uppumaanga* (mangoes) and *chammandipodi* (a mixture of so many hot spices that it had the affectionate nickname "gunpowder"). On days when the chef felt expansive, there was fried *maanthal* (dried anchovies) to go with the kanji.

The water stored in big kerosene plastic cans was so precious that Suleiman kept a close eye on it, and it was rationed out. It had to last for however long it took to arrive and unload the unhappy cargo of men and get back, dodging the radar of security forces. Abisullah was good with the fishing pole; every now and then he would be lucky enough to catch a silvery mackerel or two. He would douse them with plenty of chili powder and fry them, so every man could get a sliver of fish to go along with their rice.

Along the coast of Karachi, as the little dhow continued its undulating journey, Suleiman was suddenly alert. The boat was bouncing more than usual in the wake of what could only be a bigger vessel coming through. The smuggler's crafty eyes spotted a border patrol cutter coming their way, and he issued rapid commands.

He and Abisullah quickly managed to get their passengers to lie down in the middle of the boat and pulled a tarpaulin over them. Some supplies were positioned on top of this human cargo. Then, the smuggler and his assistant casually placed themselves at strategic points in the boat; they looked like fishermen casting poles into the water.

CHAPTER 15

When the cutter came within shouting distance, the small dhow was literally weaving up and down in the waves. Suleiman took the initiative. In a voice that oozed camaraderie he called out, "Salaam Alekkum, Machli sab kuch kaham he? Hum ko kuch bhee nahi milthe. Inshallah, kuch time ke baad voh aayegi." ("May peace be with you, where are all the fish gone? God willing, after some time they might come back.")

Reassured by the familiar greetings from the small boat, and with a sympathetic hand wave from its deck, the bigger boat moved on. The tension eased, and everyone came out from under the tarpaulin.

Having escaped another narrow detection, Suleiman was in an expansive mood. He related stories of how he had come close to being apprehended by the authorities of the various countries whose waters he sailed through with casual disregard for any kind of law. He was a law unto himself! "Njammande kazhuthe poyaalum, vellorem sahaayikkaanne vichaariche erengi porapettathalle," the great humanitarian declared. ("Even if I lose my neck, I felt like I could help a few people.")

He continued the story. "The last time I was in these waters a couple of weeks ago, I thought it was the end, because a police patrol boat came so close I was sure they would apprehend me. But at the last minute they veered off course, and I realized that they were after the high-powered smuggling boat that had passed me a few minutes before."

His passengers listened in awe at the hair-raising adventures of Suleiman on the High Seas. He told them that the return journey after they landed would be even more perilous, because he would be carrying smuggled gold. "Ellaa raajyakkaarkkum ponne venam, athilalle kaashollu." ("All the countries want gold, that's where the money is.")

Meanwhile, the seas were getting choppy and the little boat was tossed about like a child's toy. The bow would lift at such an unnatural angle it seemed like they were a hair's breadth away from capsizing.

Hanif Mohamed was scared. Wet and miserable, he huddled in a corner as he tried to fight the sickening sensation that seemed to possess every part of him. Then waves of nausea took over, and he could barely stand to purge himself over the side of the boat.

CHAPTER 16

L*akshmi's household was in a state of excitement.* Today was the day of the *Penne Kaanal* (technically translated: "Seeing the girl"), which some wags have come to refer to as the "interview." It is a ceremony when the prospective groom, his parents, and perhaps some relatives meet the proposed girl in her home for the first time.

Nalini shouted from the kitchen, "Kutti poyi aa ummaram onne nannaayi adiche thodache itte. Aalkaare varumbo enthe vichaarikkum?" ("Girl, go and make sure that the veranda is properly swept and mopped. What will people think?")

Lakshmi knew better than to argue with her mother, especially seeing Nalini's heightened state of anxiety. She reluctantly took the broom and started absentmindedly cleaning the veranda. She could not help feeling that she was helping with her own downfall.

This was the end of the road for her. After she finished her chore, before her mother could think of something else for her to do, her kindly Ammoomma intervened. "Inne nalla ore divasalle. Avale poyi onne kuliche orungeette varatte." ("Today is a good day. Let her go and take a bath and get herself ready.")

Years of wisdom had honed Ammoomma's senses, and she was not unmindful of the young woman's plight. She herself had been married at thirteen years of age to a man fifteen years her senior, and it had been a hard road. To her country way of thinking, marriage was a pragmatic necessity, because girls had no other means of supporting themselves. Their parents certainly did not want to support them unendingly.

The idea was to palm them off on a husband, and many a parent of that generation would talk about "Ore bhaaram ozhinju. Mole kettichayachu." ("It is one load off of me. I have married my daughter off.")

Nalini was busy with preparations in the kitchen. She was frying *bondas* (potato balls) and *methu vada* (savory lentil doughnuts), and a sweet item, *pazham pori* (sweet plantain fritters). All this, along with a good cup of coffee, would constitute an appropriate repast for the Penne Kaanal ceremony.

As Lakshmi sat in her room drying her long hair after a dip in the pond with an *eezharathorthe* (a thin cheesecloth-like cotton towel, extremely absorbent, yet easy to dry in the heavy monsoons of Kerala), she heard footsteps at her window.

Drawing back the curtains, Lakshmi was happy to see Divya's friendly face. "Korache notse kondannittunde tto. Nee veshamikkandirikke, ellam shariyaavum. Chekkanendaa joli?" ("I have brought you some math notes. Don't worry, everything will work out. What is the boy's job?")

Lakshmi's eyes grew wet when she explained that the prospective groom had a bachelor's in commerce and was a bank clerk. Divya nodded as she helped Lakshmi dress through the bars of the window. "Aa violet sari uduthaa mathi. Nalla udippunde. Matching potte thode." ("Just wear that violet sari. That looks nice and bright. Why don't you wear your bindi to match the sari.")

Young as she was, Divya knew the angst her friend was going through, and was determined to be supportive. When Lakshmi finished dressing, Divya clapped her hands in glee. "Cinema thaarathine vettikkum, athra sundariyaayittunde, chekkan thala karangi veenolum! Ini ende mole onne chiriche ninnaa mathi. Naale ennode ella visheshom prayanam." ("You look even better than a movie star. You look so beautiful the boy is going to faint at the sight of you. You just have to smile and pose. You need to tell me all about it when I come tomorrow.") With these encouraging words, Divya ran off.

Around four-thirty in the evening, the prospective groom arrived in a hired taxi with his parents and his sister. The broker Narankutty led the way.

Shankaran stood on the veranda to welcome the guests. He called to the back of the house: "Nalini, onne vegam vanne. Ithaaraa vannekkanenne nokkie." ("Nalini, come quickly, see who all are here.") Lakshmi's mother ran out of the kitchen wiping her forehead, which was dripping with sweat from all the frying she was doing.

Narankutty quickly made the introductions. When he came to the boy, he put his hand on the prospective groom's shoulder like he was showing off a prize cattle and beamed. "Ithaa njaan paranja chekkan. Bankile claarkaa!" ("This is the boy I was talking about. He is a clerk in the bank!") The message was clear: The young man had a bachelor's in commerce and held a clerical position in Vijaya bank in the next town. He was a good catch, so don't blow it.

They sat down and went through the rituals of the ceremony. Each side tried to take stock of the other without seeming to do so, and to learn something about the other side that had not been documented in the dossier.

The boy's name was Mohan, and his folks were quick to drop hints about the many cents (minute fractions of an acre) of paddy fields and coconut trees they owned, leaving no doubt about the financial security of their family. Between holding forth about their various assets, the father of the prospective groom tried to pry out of Shankaran what further earthly possessions he might own.

The idea was to get as much material wealth from the bride's party as possible, thus ensuring their son's future. You could tell they were disappointed at Shankaran's limited means. The background checks being over, the father of the groom announced condescendingly, "Aappo ini pennum cherukkanum onne kaanatte, alle." ("Now we should let the girl and boy see each other, right?")

Shankaran nodded to Nalini, who promptly fetched Lakshmi. From her room, Lakshmi had gotten a good look at the boy as he got out of the car. She was dismayed that he seemed barely to reach her height!

He was plump and short. His pants appeared to almost burst at the seams, and his fair skin seemed to accentuate a certain softness about him. So when her mother called her to the kitchen and handed her the tray with the tea and *palahaarams* (sweet treats) she had spent all morning making, Lakshmi took it to the veranda with a sense of resignation.

CHAPTER 16

Shankaran was at his genial best. As she handed the visitors glasses of tea, he announced, "Aa ithaane ende mole Lakshmi." ("This is my daughter, Lakshmi.")

The prospective mother-in-law paid close attention to how the girl approached the party. Looking for any defects in her gait and finding none, she asked Lakshmi in her sweetest voice, "Collegile endaane subjecte?" ("What is your subject in college?") This was more to ensure that the girl had a reasonable voice than any great interest in her scholastic aptitude.

Lakshmi answered modestly.

Her father, as a concession to modern youthful frivolities, proudly said, "Cherukkane vallathum chothikaanundengi chothikkaalo!" ("If the boy has something to ask the girl, he should feel free to do so.") But the prospective groom, Mohan, just looked down and smiled. After tea, the groom's party said their goodbyes, climbed into the taxi, and were gone.

Lakshmi's household was in a state of anxious anticipation as to whether their daughter was acceptable to the groom and his family. Whatever Lakshmi's private feelings were, Shankaran and his wife thought the boy was a good catch with a well-paying job. Ammoomma and Amma practically raved about him. "Nalla eishwaryam olla mukhaa. Endaa neram!" ("He has a very cultured face, and he certainly is fair!") When asked how she felt about him, Lakshmi gave an indifferent shrug, which seemed to irritate them.

The next day, Narankutty returned. One look at his face told the parents all they needed to know—the boy's people had rejected the proposal. The broker held nothing back. "Kuttikke aanungale pole pokkam. Nerom korache koravaa. Pinne veettile valia sthithi onnum indenne thonnanilla." ("The girl is almost as tall as most men. And she is not very fair. And we don't think that they have much wealth to speak of.")

It was a disappointment to Shankaran and Nalini, and their faces showed it. But ever the optimist, the broker was on to the next case. "Angane vari adikkaanonnum illenne. Kadalile mathi pole ineem venda cherukkanmarille namakke." ("There is nothing that much to worry about. Like sardines in the sea, there are plenty of boys to choose from.") He picked up his umbrella and the sacred black book of prospective names, saw himself out of the house, and left through the gate.

They say that hope springs eternal in the human heart. After a month with no news from Narankutty, Lakshmi's parents started to worry again. Without too much money to give, and a girl who was tall and dark-skinned, they knew their chances of finding a real catch of a groom were extremely slim.

As anxiety gave way to despair, Lakshmi's father grew more peevish by the minute. He found fault with everything she did: his shirt was never ironed well enough, the curries Lakshmi prepared lacked salt or chilis or both, and he was irritated by her attempts at continuing her education by reading the books Divya brought her.

"Padiche padiche, doctorate eduthitte oraalivide irikkanille, ninde oru kemi mole!" ("Your daughter has studied so hard, she must be a PhD by now, your clever daughter!") This was directed at Nalini, who felt bad for Lakshmi, the object of all of her father's frustrations in life.

At this juncture Narankutty paid another visit to the Shankaran household. As if he had handled an Israeli-Palestinian peace talk, he informed Shankaran: "Nammale kodukkana thoga avarkke virodalya. Kutty korache adjuste cheyyanamenne ollu.

Pinne nammade mumbile chowaadoshalle nikkane." ("They will be satisfied with the amount you are prepared to give. The girl might have to adjust a little bit. After all, we are saddled with the astrological defect of Chowwadosham.")

After that, Lakshmi could hear no more from the other room, since they were speaking in whispered tones. Seeing her parents' desperation gave her a great deal of anxiety. On the day of the next Penne Kaanal, Lakshmi looked out of the window with trepidation. A taxi pulled up at their small gate. Two men, a thirty-something young lady, and a plump middle-aged woman came through the gate.

The gentleman with gray hair, presumably the father, walked slowly, doubtless so that the younger man with a prominent limp could keep up with him. The young man projected a general air of irritability; he seemed to be scowling. Her heart sank. The young woman was pretty. She and the older woman were looking around, taking stock of their surroundings.

Shankaran was all smiles as he ushered them into chairs arranged on the veranda. "Varanam, varanam, veede kande pidikkaan budhimuttundaayo?" ("Come, come, and sit down, did you have any trouble finding the house?")

The usual pleasantries dealt with, Lakshmi got her usual summons from her father to come before the distinguished gathering.

Seeing the young lady standing before him in all her vulnerability, the kindly old man acknowledged her. "Ide ende mon Satheeshan.Panchaayat offeecilaane joli.Government udyogathile vigalaangarkke sowjanyam undallo." ("This is my son, Satheeshan. He works in the Panchaayat office. Because it is a government job, he gets preference for his handicap!")

The boy looked down, and his mother gave her husband a seething look for having divulged her son's disability in this public manner. Undeterred, the old man bumbled on, "Satheeshan, my son, is there anything you would like to say to this young lady? If there is something in particular you would like to ask her, this is the time."

The young man seemed to have a perpetual grimace on his face. "I am not very keen on my wife working outside of the home. The husband can bring home the income, and the wife can keep the home going. It has worked for my parents, and that is how I wish to proceed," he blurted out. The men on the veranda nodded in unison at the young man's wise words.

Before Lakshmi could say anything, her mother answered for her. "Athine ivalkum veette kaaryam nokki nadakkanaa thaalparyam. Ividethe pennungalaarum porathe jolikke poyittilya." ("That is our daughter's wish as well. She prefers to be a housewife. No woman in this household has gone outside of the house to work.")

This seemed to satisfy the groom's family. As they got into their taxi and drove off, Lakshmi gave her mother a venomous look. "What is wrong with his foot? He was limping the whole time!"

Her father explained, "It's nothing to fret about. He was born with a club foot."

Her mother looked into the stormy eyes of her daughter and said, "Penninde ore negalam, pinne Vijayashree alle." ("Look at the vanity of the girl, as if she is the film star Vijayashree herself!")

CHAPTER 17

The day of the wedding, the heavens opened in an uncharacteristic downpour, as if drenching the earth with its tears.

The guests asked in perplexity, "Ende eeshwaraa, ee kodum venalkaalathe ingane oru mazha! Lakshanam nannilla." ("Dear God, how can it rain so hard in the middle of this scorching summer! This is not a good sign.")

As the newly married couple touched the feet of each elderly relative, asking for their blessings, the guests shook their heads and threw rice on the couple's heads.

Lakshmi went through it all with resignation. She was used to not getting all that she wanted. Even when Divya and Lakshmi's cousin Preethy braided her hair and wound it with strands of jasmine, she sat as still as a statue with an impassive face—a goddess Lakshmi carved in stone.

At the temple, even as they exchanged garlands, the groom was still scowling. The bride and groom did not utter a single word to each other. The reception was held in the small courtyard of Shankaran's house where a *pandal* (a tent with a thatched roof) had been erected, and long school tables and benches were arranged.

The village cook had come to prepare the vegetarian *Sadhya* (feast), which was hastily served on banana leaves placed on the tables. People ate quickly and waited for the dessert, a banana and a dollop of *paayasam* (vermicelli pudding). The guests went through that in record time as well. Afterwards, they carefully folded their banana leaves and discarded them in a pit made for that purpose.

A cup of steaming hot tea served in small, crude industrial strength glasses, and *paan* (a betel leaf mixture) completed the meal. After the older guests finished, the last group to sit for lunch were Lakshmi's friends from the parallel college. Divya, Keerthi, Arathi, Sumithra, and Rajalakshmi wore their best sarees, and even some of the boys from Lakshmi's class had come to wish her happiness.

Lakshmi's heart was full when she saw the familiar goofy faces of Ravi, Javed, Bashir, and Saleem. She longed to ask them what had happened to Hanif Mohamad. She had heard from Divya that he had left in a smuggler's boat to seek his fortunes in Dubai. But now that she was a married lady, the question died in her throat.

Nevertheless, they were still young people who enjoyed each other's company. When lunch was served, the girls giggled uncontrollably at the huge amounts of rice and curries the boys asked the servers to replenish their plates with. Just when the servers thought they would never finish, the young people, having thoroughly enjoyed their meal, went to wash their hands.

Just before they left, they gave Lakshmi a wedding present: a mechanical monkey that, when wound up, could scratch itself,

CHAPTER 17

and go through the motions of eating a banana. "Just to remind you of us monkeys," they said as they handed her the gift.

Watching Lakshmi try to work the mechanism sent the young people into hysterical laughter. Suddenly, Lakshmi felt young again, and her mood lightened. Many times during her marriage, she would take out the monkey and gaze at it to remind her that she had indeed been carefree at one time.

Her parents had vacated their bigger bedroom so the couple could spend their first night as man and wife in the comfort of the only decent bedroom in the house. When Lakshmi entered the room with the customary glass of warm milk, Satheeshan was sitting on the bed in his *lunghi* (nighttime dhoti). He had changed out of his wedding clothes, taken a bath, and was waiting for her.

Lakshmi smiled tentatively, extended her hand, and offered him the glass of milk. Wordlessly he took it, drank the whole glass, and set it on the table. He motioned for her to sit on the bed. An embarrassed silence grew between them. To break it, she haltingly remarked, "Endore mazhayaayirunnu alle, sari muzhuvan nananju!" ("What a downpour it was, wasn't it? My whole sari got wet!") Even at this tentative attempt at conversation, his expression remained irritated.

Then he asked her a question that threw her off. "Kutti ethra vare padichu? Endaa paditham nirthiye? ("How many years did you go to college? Why did you suddenly stop your education?") It was the last question she had expected to hear this early in the marriage.

"Rande kollam parallel collegile poyi, math aayirunnu vishayam," she replied vaguely. ("I attended the parallel college for two years. My subject was mathematics.")

"Hmm, we also heard some stories about why you stopped your education. We didn't pay too much credence to it. After all, any stupid boy can give any girl a love letter, although why he would choose you is another matter. And today I saw you with your so-called friends, talking and laughing with boys. It is behavior totally unacceptable for a bride. The women in my house are always well behaved in public, and I hope you will follow their example in the way you conduct yourself."

Lakshmi was stung by the pettiness of his statement and felt defensive. "Koode padicha kuttiolode varthaanam paranjathe vellia kola kuttam onnum alla!" ("Talking to one's own college classmates is not exactly a capital offense!")

He replied with sarcasm, "Let me make it plain. I expect my wife to behave with more decorum than that! Don't think that I was hard up to get a bride because of my foot and the astrological disadvantage. We had so many proposals to choose from, and it was based on the broker's assurance that we went with you. Don't make our family regret the decision."

Lakshmi had to bite her tongue from asking, "What prevented you from marrying anyone else? I wasn't exactly pining for you, either!" Instead, she went to the bathroom, carefully took off her beautiful sari, and fastidiously folded it.

One by one, she took the strands of jasmine flowers from her hair and placed them on the windowsill. When she undid her braids, her long hair fell in cascades around her shoulders, down to the back of her knees. She changed into her modest cotton nightie and came back to bed.

It was as if a wall separated the two sides of the marital bed. He had fallen asleep. So she lay down on her side of the bed, and with a sigh of resignation, covered her body with the sheet that served as a blanket. She woke in the middle of the night with the weight of someone on top of her, feeling her all over. His breathing came in shallow grunts and as he roughly entered her. In a couple of minutes it was over. He rolled onto his side of the bed, found a comfortable position, and fell into a slumber.

The girl was left with a sharp sensation of pain and an unfathomable feeling of emptiness. Once more, she pulled the sheet up to her chin and tried to go back to sleep. Once more, she realized that this was not a path that would be easy to navigate.

Mercifully, like a blanket of snow covering the tired earth, sleep overcame her, and the events of the day receded into the background.

CHAPTER 18

By *the fourth day at sea*, a kind of monotony had set in. Listlessness enveloped the men, who clung to their big dreams in a promised land. Hanif Mohamed was slowly getting used to the rhythm of the boat, his stomach slowly settling down. He felt like a sponge wrung dry of all emotions and feelings. There were times when all he could do was vomit, leaning over the edge of the boat. Once or twice, when it looked like he might keel over into the sea with exhaustion, one of the others held onto him.

It was camaraderie among *Les Misérables*, who understood that they needed each other to survive in the little floating vessel taking them to Dubai.

In the long hours that stretched before them, each one had heard the miserable stories of the others—stories of unwanted births, fortunes frittered away, the breakdown of families, and, sometimes, as in the case of Hanif Mohamed, a misguided love affair.

CHAPTER 18

They told these stories in monotones, like men who had lost their faith in humanity, and hence did not want to attribute warmth and emotion to their pasts.

Jaafar, the oldest of the group, was the victim of a business deal gone bad—with his closest buddy. His land, home, and all his wife's ornaments had been taken as collateral for his debts. The family was forced to take refuge with his parents, who were understandably unhappy about the situation.

He said, "Businessile nannaayitte alochichitte venam kootte koodaan. Allenghi chathiche naashaakkum!" ("You need to be very careful who you enter into business partnerships with. Otherwise, they can cheat you and destroy you!") He imparted this wisdom with an expansive gesture of his hand. The others, who had never attempted to venture even that far out in life, were impressed. Collectively, they felt sorry for him.

Then there was Jamaal, a young man with sensitive features who was withdrawn and shy. He sat at one end of the boat with his head hanging down, saying hardly anything. His misfortune seemed only to emphasize how unfit he was for this trip. His family had married him to a beautiful girl whose attentions had soon turned towards another. Her lover had a motorcycle and a leather jacket, and his hair was greased back with coconut oil into a high pompadour. This rival's manly ways and slick talk had attracted her to him.

Then, while Jamaal was away at work in a stationary shop, the flirting had progressed into something more. Jamaal was the object of derision among the men in his town. They told him, "Ninakke ninde pennine onne nelakke nirthikoode? Kali koodi koodi evede chennethaanaa?" ("Can't you control your wife? Where is this going to end?")

Whenever he tried to broach the subject with his beloved, even in the most tentative of ways, she threw such a tantrum that he hastily retreated into his shell. Then one fine day, he returned from work to find her gone, along with all her things and the money he had been putting away so carefully in a little iron box for a rainy day.

It was the last straw in a series of humiliations, and once more he stood in front of his Vappa, this time to borrow money to embark on this journey.

❈

There was an ease with which the men recounted these stories in the company of others who had suffered similar fates. They did not judge each other and tried to support one another. They hoped their destination would bring them opportunities to get ahead in life and help them leave their pasts behind.

The undulating waves of the Arabian Sea carried their little life raft forward, towards their goal. The murky deep water had witnessed many a tear. It churned as if it was trying to dissolve all the human misery that passed through it.

Suleiman took his duties as captain seriously. While he tried not to get entangled in the passenger's personal lives, he felt a certain responsibility for their collective fate. He had come up from nothing. Although as a smuggler he was used to taking chances, and he could take down anybody who threatened him, he felt paternal towards this boatload of misfits, most of whom shared his faith.

As the experienced world traveller, he was also their fund of information on all things pertaining to Dubai. In his own way he tried to ground them in the reality they would face after getting off the boat.

CHAPTER 18

"Aa avide poomaala itte sweegarikkaan velcome committee onnum indaavilla ketta. Kittana joli eduthe jeevikkaan nokke. Pinne korache kaashe maatti veche, padukke kara keraan nokke. Vellia vazhakkinum, strikinum onnum ponda. Vegam vandi ketti vidum. Athokke keralele vechitte poyaa mathi. Pinne njaan ende pattanathile vellia judgy aayirunnu ennokke paranje vellia udyogam nokki irunnaa pattini aavum. Kittana thozhil nannaayi cheyyaan nokke." ("Don't expect any welcoming committee waiting to garland you on the other side. Take whatever job you can get. Then put aside a little money and try to establish yourself. Don't go in for strikes and other fights. This is the surest way to be deported. Leave that behind in Kerala. Don't go around telling everyone you were a big shot in your hometown, and don't be expecting some highfalutin job, or you will go hungry. Whatever job you get, try to do it well.")

There were years of wisdom and experience behind these words. In his many years as a smuggler and human trafficker, Suleiman had seen people fail too often due to unrealistic expectations.

"Avide chennaa ningalke bandhookkaare arengilum illenghi, nere Safa parkilekke poyko. Avide ore moolele ningalkum koodaam. Saadhaarana kettida paniyaa kittaa. Eluppandaavilla, nalla chutta veyilathe paniyaan. Chelappa avare shambalam tharaandirikkaan nokkum. Athe enganeyengilum vaangikkanam. Pinne nannaayi adwaaniche keripogaan nokke. Allah ningade koode indaagatte. Inshallah!" ("When you reach there, if you don't have relatives to stay with, go straight to Safa Park. You can find a place in a corner there. Construction jobs are the most common you will get. It's not going to be easy working in the burning hot sun. And sometimes they will try to shortchange you out of your salary. Make sure you get your wages. Work hard and try to better yourself. Allah will be with you. God willing!")

He was referring to Dubai's infamous Safa Park, the temporary refuge for all migrant workers. It was derisively called the "plywood city" because of its hastily constructed shacks, where men—and sometimes women and children—lived close together in squalor and poverty. Discarded timber from the construction sites was the only material used to build these lean-to homes. With no electricity and running water, the sanitation was poor, and when darkness fell, the sea of tents was illuminated with kerosene lamps. The smell of kerosene and the feeble light of these lamps were the only Arabian night tales these unfortunate people experienced after landing there.

The group listened intently. This was the first time any of them had travelled this far from home, and to a foreign land where the people and customs were alien, and their language unknown. Their feelings ran the gamut of extreme anxiety to nervousness, from cautious hope to muted excitement at a new beginning, however dangerous it sounded.

As the seventh day approached, one could literally see the tension building in Suleiman. This was the most dangerous part of the operation. Everything had to work like clockwork, and things could go wrong in a minute. He prepared his passengers one more time.

"Inne raathri njaan paranja aa cheria dweepile chennethum. Vellathinde naduvile kale kuthaan ore cheriya sthalam enne karuthiyaa mathi. Avide kondethichaa ende chomathala theernnu. Karakkaduthaa police pidikkum. Avidenne ore rande milolam varum beachilekke. Ellaarkkum neendaan ariyaamennalle paranje. Neendi rakshapeduga. Policinde kannee pedaande nokkikko. Chelappo jolikkaare anweshiche truck varum. Kerippoyi adwaniche jeevikkaan nokke. Inshallah!"

("Tonight we will reach the small island I talked about. Think of it as a little foothold in the middle of the ocean. When we reach there, my responsibilities towards you will end. If I get closer to the shore, the police will catch me. The beach is about two miles from there. All of you have assured me that you can swim. This is your chance to swim and get to a new life. Try not to get noticed by the police. Sometimes you will see trucks by the beachside, looking for workers for the construction sites. Get on one of them, work hard, and make something of yourselves, God willing!")

They arrived at their destination by late afternoon. Hanif Mohamed could not believe how tenuous a foothold it was—a piece of land no bigger than a house in the middle of the Arabian Sea. It looked as if even the ocean did not want to claim it. From time immemorial, this had been a gateway for countless immigrants seeking their fortunes in the city of gold—their Ellis Island.

They pulled the boat onto dry land, lowered the masts to prevent detection, and waited. When darkness fell and a sliver of moon lit up the night sky, the smuggler instructed the men to start swimming.

Like so many minnows in the water, they made their way towards the beach. The smuggler would wait on the island; his cargo of gold would be rowed out to him sometime during the night. He and Abisullah would run it across the Arabian Sea back to Kerala, and under the cover of night, bury it in assigned places on the seashore where his patrons knew to find it.

Suleiman prided himself on being a professional. He had never once been caught by the Coast Guard or the police. Yet he could not get rid of a certain primordial anxiety when he watched the men swimming in desperation.

He had seen it all—the simple ones get picked up by the police, and some who drowned. Yet he had seen fierce determination in the faces of some of these men he had ferried. With his years of experience, he could almost pick out who would succeed, and who would end up exactly where he left them.

It was difficult, even for a seasoned smuggler like him, not to be moved by the desperate human beings wrung by hunger, seasickness, and dread of the unknown, valiantly swimming ashore with no clue as to the outcome.

People say human beings live on love, but human beings really live on faith—the faith of hope that tomorrow will turn out better than today.

CHAPTER 19

Divya *was thrilled that Lakshmi had married* someone whose job did not require him to move to another town. This meant she could see her childhood friend whenever she wanted to, although she always made sure that Lakshmi's husband, Satheeshan, was not around when she visited. He did not look like a particularly friendly man.

Lakshmi and her husband had moved into a small one-bedroom house. A lean-to shack at its side was meant to be a convenience for Satheeshan to park his scooter, so he (and it) would not get wet during the monsoons.

Nalini and Shankaran visited to preside over the milk boiling over (housewarming) ceremony. When the new milk boiled over the sides of a pot, crusting on the stove, everyone declared it a sign of prosperity, and that the house had good *lakshanam* (omen).

As was the custom, Lakshmi's parents had furnished the house with a bed, a wardrobe, and a small dining table with chairs. Satheeshan's mother was still not satisfied. She implied that she had had to provide a lot more when it was her daughter's turn. The bride's parents had also brought with them the essential kitchen utensils—a big pot for cooking rice, a couple of smaller ones for milk and tea, a nice *cheena chatty* (the traditional Kerala wok copied from the Chinese), some of the necessary *kaile* (spatulas), and some steel eating vessels such as plates and glasses.

Lakshmi's mother-in-law stuck her head into the kitchen. With an appraising glance that took in everything, she declared, "Sowgaryangale okke korache koravaanalle. Pinne aalkaarude vichaaram makkale kettichayachaa chomathala okke theernoonna! Pinne valla cherukkandem bhaaraaville." ("There are hardly any conveniences here. But then, parents think that once they have married off their daughter they have no further obligations towards her! Then it becomes the bridegroom's load to bear.")

This was an arrow aimed at Lakshmi's parents, who looked away at being labeled delinquent providers. The wedding ceremony, along with the trousseau and the dowry, had just about wiped out all the money they had obtained from selling the small piece of land adjacent to their house.

Later, back in her own house, Nalini bristled at the implied insult by Lakshmi's mother-in-law. "Aa saadhanam muzhuvan vaangiche koduthitte athine poraanne. Vellia panakkaarithiyalle, vaangiche kodukkaayirunnille, njaan vendaanne paranjo?" ("After buying all those things for the house, she dares to say it is not enough. The great rich woman could have bought her some more things if she wanted to, I did not stop her, did I?") But for her daughter's sake, and to ensure that there would be future peace in the house, Nalini held her tongue around the mother-in-law.

Life in the new household fell into a daily rhythm. Lakshmi got up each morning and bathed in cold water, then prepared her husband's breakfast. She would make *idlis* (rice cakes) or *dosa* (thin pancakes) from batter she had ground on the stone the night before and left out on the kitchen counter to ferment. Besides breakfast, lunch also had to be prepared in the morning so that Satheeshan could carry his lunch to work. She would hurriedly put the rice on and cut vegetables for the curry. Satheeshan did not like to bathe in cold water, and hence, one stove was dedicated to heating up water in a large pot for his bath.

Using two pieces of cloth, Lakshmi would painstakingly pick up this hot pot, hurry to the bathroom and empty it in the bucket there. Satheeshan would get mad if the water was not just the right temperature, so Lakshmi made sure it was as he liked it.

She was becoming used to his irritability and nastiness, although the acidity of his words could hurt her feelings. He was the fussiest about food. Lakshmi learned early that his words and his temper were equally dreadful.

One morning, when she put a steaming plate of idlis with chutney in front of him, he took one bite, then flung the plate at her, shouting, "Chutneele uppidaan aarum ninne padippiche thannille, manushane vaayele vekkaan kollaatha oronne indaakki tharaan ore bhaarya! Vellia padippe kaarialle, athinalle samayollu." ("Didn't anyone teach you how to put salt in the chutney, making food unfit for human consumption—that is the duty of a wife! But of course, she is a great scholar, and that is all she has time for.")

He was referring to how in the afternoon, when all was quiet and Lakshmi had finished her chores, she would try to go through some of the books that Divya had given her. This irritated Satheeshan; he often made barbed comments about it. Lakshmi *had* forgotten to put salt in the chutney, and the next hour was spent cleaning up the food that had splattered on the floor and the walls.

Today, Lakshmi was excited. Divya had come by the house the previous afternoon with a couple of books and something new for Lakshmi—a bright red cutex (nail polish). She was brimming with excitement about the new movie she had seen at the Jose theatre the previous afternoon.

"Prem Nazeerum, Sheelem, Vijayashreeyum okke inde. Abhinayam ugranaayittinde. Paattum nallathaa. Angerode konde pogaan chodikke" ("Prem Nazeer, Sheela, and Vijayashree are all acting in it. The acting is superb. The songs are also very good. Tell him to take you for it.")

After dinner that evening, Lakshmi tentatively approached Satheeshan when he was relaxing on the veranda with his feet up. She did not mention that Divya had told her about the movie because he did not like Lakshmi's friendship with her; he thought the other girl too forward.

"Ore puthiya cinema vannittunde. Ivide kaarile viliche parayanundaayirunnu. Nalla padaane. Enne onne kondu pogo?" ("A new movie has come to town. They were advertising it with a loudspeaker from a car. It sounds like a good movie. Will you take me for it?")

He must have been in a good mood, for without too much argument, he agreed to take her to the seven o'clock show the next evening.

That night, Lakshmi quickly gave Satheeshan his tea, and even made his favorite *pazham pori* (banana fritters) as a snack. Then she took a bath, carefully dressed in a yellow sari, and braided her hair, adorning it with a couple of jasmine buds from the garden. With great care, she applied the cutex to her fingernails, and admired them while blowing on them to dry. She felt beautiful. As she stepped onto the veranda, Satheeshan was closing and bolting the various doors. When he turned around to look at her, his reaction was not what she had hoped for.

"Idendaanithe, kayyilum kaalilumokke paintadiche, endaa kallu shappinde aduthe poyi nikkaanaa, ee maathiri vesham kettiyekkane?" ("What is all this, painting your hands and feet? Are you planning to go and stand near the toddy shop to pick up some customers dressed like this?")

Lakshmi cringed. She was sure that would be the end of the movie, but thankfully, Satheeshan started walking towards the bus stand, and she meekly followed. There was a long line at the ticket counter outside the theatre. Satheeshan took his place in the line with Lakshmi by his side. As they waited their turn, a group of rowdy young people made their way towards the entrance. As they passed them, one guy looked Lakshmi up and down and whistled in appreciation. Another Romeo felt the desire to sing a line from his favorite movie: "Njaan ninne premikkunnu maan kidaave, manasil paathi pakuthe tharu . . ." ("I am in love with you, my beautiful fawn, please let me have at least half of your heart . . .")

Satheeshan exploded. "Nningalkonnum vere thozhilille, vellorudem pennungale upadravikaanallaande? ("Don't you have anything else to do other than bother someone else's women?") The young Turks, confident in their youth and numbers, were not about to back off.

"Ee kelavende ore chorichile? Ivide paadaan paadillanne neyamam onnum illallo? Thaan ivarude appanaayirikkum alle. Wheel onne pancharaayaalum, kelavande ore mooche!" ("Why is this old man so irritable? Is there any rule saying that we cannot sing? You must be her father, is that right? One wheel is punctured, but look at the temper of the old man!") This last was a callous reference to Satheeshan's clubfoot.

The boys knew very well that he was the woman's husband, but they were itching for a fight. Satheeshan knew it was not to his advantage to start one, so, dragging Lakshmi by the hand, they returned home. Once there, he was unable to simmer down—and it was all Lakshmi's fault.

"Ippo manasilaayo, vellia lokaika sundarikke, ingane paintokke adiche veshyagale pole porathe nadakkumbe endaa indaavaanne?" ("Now does the great Miss World understand what happens when you paint yourself like a whore and walk on the streets?")

CHAPTER 20

*A*likka, *as he was affectionately called*, was taking an early morning stroll along the beach with his trusted right-hand man, Asseem. They were discussing ways to meet the increasing demand among the migrant population for native Malayali food, the ever-increasing cost of doing business, and the problems small-time employers like himself ran into when employing migrant workers.

"Kambolathile saadhanangalkokke mudinja vela alle. Pinne bhakshanam thucha velakke kittem venam. Ithe randum enganyaa othe povaa?" ("In the market, the prices of things have skyrocketed. And everyone wants to eat at low cost. How do both these things go together?")

This was Ali, the proprietor of Kerala Canteen, speaking of the woes of running a business in Dubai. He had come in the '50s in a small *Kalla thoni* (smuggler's boat). His leathery skin, the deep grooves on his face, and his callused hands were a testament to what he had been through to arrive here. Sheer grit and determination, and, for a small man, an uncanny ability to work hard and seize an opportunity when it came, had gotten him to where he was now.

Asseem had great admiration for his boss, and could read what was on Alikka's mind.

"Aa puthiya chekkane naattee ponamenne ore vichaaram maathraane. Vellia transistarum, onne rande nalla nerolla sareem, ore sorna pavanum, korache roopem kayyee pidichethiyaa avane avade raajaavaakkumennaa vichaaram. Joli eduthe thodangumbazhekkum avande avagaashangalokke erakkeettunde. Pinne Sheikh innale vannirinnu. Vaadaka chelappo koottumenna thonnane. Njelinjirunne kai neettiyaa matheelo, one." ("That new fellow we hired can think only of when he can return to Kerala. He thinks if he shows up there with a transistor radio and a couple of gaudy sarees, a gold coin, and a few rupees in his pocket, he will be welcomed like a king. Even before they start their work, their entitlements are a mile long. And by the way, the Sheik came by yesterday. I have a feeling he is going to increase our rent. Of course, he just has to sit in his comfortable armchair and extend his hand our way.")

Asseem was referring to the practice in the Middle East of not allowing migrants to own property. The only way they could start a business was to partner with a local Emirati. This ensured a steady income for the local citizen as he collected rent from the business. It was a feudal system where the businesses worked hard to stay in the good books of their landlords or face eviction and have one's visa revoked.

For Ali and Asseem, after putting in their daily orders at the market and instructing their crew to transport it to the canteen kitchen and begin meal prep, their time on the beach was their

CHAPTER 20

quiet time away from the nosy employees to take in some fresh air and discuss business.

This was only a brisk thirty minute walk by the seashore, good for clearing the head and putting things in perspective. Sometimes it was a time to reminisce about how they had arrived fifteen years earlier, scrawny, hungry, and desperate. They could be seen laughing about how they made it across the small stretch of ocean where the smuggler had dropped them off, when neither of them knew how to swim and they drank plenty of saltwater in the process of reaching land.

Suddenly, Alikka stopped. Pointing to a little mound in the sand, he said, "Edaa Asseeme', aa manale anangana kandaa. Padachone, athinde adeele alindenna thonnane! Vegam vaadaa!" ("Hey, Asseem, did you see that mound of sand moving! Allah, I think there is a man under there! Come quickly!")

Alikka ran towards the mound, and Asseem tried to keep up. With his hands, Alikka frantically removed the sand from the human form under it. It was the figure of a young man. He lay perfectly still, and Alikka fretted that he was too late.

"Asseeme, aa water bottlele vellam ingotte thanne. Neriya shwaasam indenna thonnane." ("Asseem, just pass me the water bottle. I think I detect a little breathing.")

With that, the older man washed the sand from the face of the boy on the beach. He cradled the head and tried to get the boy to drink some water. As soon as the water went down his throat, the young man started to cough, probably from all the saltwater he had swallowed and the sand that had worked its way into his mouth as he lay unconscious.

"Ikka, kadelethanam, allenghi avanmarokke, kaiyyum ketti irikkindaavum, ore paneem edukkaande.Vallorum vanne kooli velakke koottikonde poykolum, vareen." ("Big brother, we need to get to the shop, or the workers will be sitting there with their hands folded, doing nothing. Someone will come around and take him for construction work. Let's go.")

Alikka was still trying to revive the young man with water. He was rewarded when the man showed signs of wanting to sit up. Alikka was a true Muslim; he had lost track of how many immigrants he had given a leg up to. Many would go on their way to prosperity and never give a backward glance to the man who gave them a break. But every now and then, he was surprised to be met with gratitude by someone who had done well for himself after getting his first break from him.

"Nee poyi pani thodange, njaanippo ethaam. Gathi mutti nilkumbo aasha koduthitte, avanmarokke ithungale chaala kottana mathiri thattiyitte povum. Ivane kanditte endo nalla veetteennanne thonnane. Rakshapeduthaan pattonne ore kai nokkatte. Pinne nammallum ingane okke vannathalle! Padachon ennode aavashyapedane pole ore thonnalaa. Nee poyko." ("Why don't you go and start the work, I'll be right there. When people are desperate, these smugglers give them false hope and then dump them like fish on these beaches. He looks like he is from a good family. Let me see if I can get him to come around. Remember, we also have travelled this same way. I feel that Allah wants me to help this guy. You go on.")

Alikka started gently patting the boy's face to bring back some circulation, and he worked his legs and arms to do the same. Asseem shook his head and walked off. This was the most infuriating part of his employer/friend: that he was ready with open arms to help most people, even good-for-nothings. But it was also the part of Alikka that made Asseem so loyal to the older man.

CHAPTER 20

Alikka would never be able to stop reaching out to other human beings in crisis. When a man hits rock bottom and slowly, by sheer will, works himself out of this hellhole (in the process seeing the worst of humanity), and yet, maybe once or twice he is privy to the nobility of another human being, his reactions in later life can go one of two ways: His earlier travails can make him a mean-spirited individual, suspicious of all and envious of those who do better—trying to hoard what he can, while he can. But then there is a rare human being, for whom the earlier hardships encountered were a lesson in humanity, in how to be a better human being. He has no illusions about how hard the world can be to the less fortunate, but ever the optimist, he chooses to focus on the few helping hands that were extended to him along the way. That becomes his mission, his purpose. It was Hanif Mohamed's luck that he happened to make land in the path of such a man.

When the water trickled down his throat, Hanif Mohamed started to cough and wretch, and he vomited on the sand. "Korachum koodi vellam kudikke. Mone ezhunnettirikkaan patto?" ("Drink a little bit more water. Do you think you can sit up now, son?")

When Hanif tried to sit up, it seemed the whole world had been upended on its axis. As the older man propped him up, slowly, the events of the previous night came back to him. When Hanif Mohamed had told the boatman he could swim, it was an overstatement borne from the fact that he had thrashed his arms and legs about in the local pond. It had nowhere near made him ready for the Arabian Sea with its undulating waves and unfathomable depth.

Under the cover of darkness, when all of them had jumped out into the sea at Suleiman's orders, he was not prepared for the constant buffeting of the waves, and the tiredness that creeps into one's arms and legs from the constant fighting with the sea that is waiting at every turn to claim you for its own.

Gafoor, who was by his side when they started the journey, was doing better. He tried to encourage Hanif Mohamed as they made their way towards the shore. "Edaa Haneefe, kaalum kayyum onnitte adichaa mathi. Athikam vellam kudikkaande nokke!" ("Hey, Hanif, just move your hands and legs, man. Try not to drink too much saltwater!")

This was easier said than done. Days of deprivation and dehydration on the boat had taken its toll, and the seasickness, with its constant vomiting, had left him with few reserves. When a big wave crashed over him and separated him from Gafoor, Hanif Mohamed wondered if he would ever make it to the shore.

In his darkest hour, when he thought it was the end, his thoughts strayed to the two people in the world whom he loved, and whose love would always be denied to him: His Umma, who had died when he was a suckling infant, and the beautiful slender girl who had captivated him. He was bidding his goodbye to the only two people who mattered in the world to him. His body was tired, and he was glad to give in to the waves that chose to carry him wherever they pleased.

Now, seated on a bench in Alikka's crowded kitchen with all its noise and bustling kitchen help, Hanif Mohamed's nostrils were aware of a familiar, overpowering smell—that of freshly made biryani when the seal of the vessel made of flour and water (called the *dhum*) is broken and the biryani is ready for serving.

CHAPTER 20

Alikka brought him a steaming plate. For Hanif, who had had only a couple of so-called meals on the boat of dried fish or pickles and rice, this was heaven. He attacked it with gusto.

Alikka chuckled. "Padukke thinne, ineem tharaam,dahana kede varum." ("Go slowly, young man, we will give you more. You are going to get indigestion at this rate.")

Alikka barked at the kitchen helper who had come to gawk at his latest charity case: "Ithe kaazhcha banglaavonnum alla, endaa manushanmaare thinnane kandittille? Poyi joli nokkada Hamukke!" ("This is not a zoo for you to gawk at, haven't you seen people eat before? Go and do your job, good-for-nothings!")

At his order, one of the assistants brought Hanif Mohamed a glass of steaming hot milky tea. It certainly hit a spot, and he was starting to feel lethargic from his adventures at sea. But politeness dictated that he wash the vessels he ate from, and as he washed his plate and glass he noticed the other dishes in the huge sink and proceeded to wash them as well. Alikka stopped him. "Adokke naaleyaavaam. Inne mon poyi kuliche kuppayokke maatti onne oranghe. Pinnethe kaaryam naale alochikkaam." ("We can do all that tomorrow. Right now, why don't you take a bath, change your clothes, and go to bed. We can think of everything else tomorrow.")

The restaurant owner instructed one of the younger kitchen help to lend Hanif a pair of his clothes, and find him a mat which he could lay out in the storeroom and sleep on. Alikka pretended not to see the tears that welled up in the young man's eyes at this unexpected kindness. He gave a curt nod when Hanif Mohamed put his right hand over his heart in the greatest acknowledgment of gratitude.

CHAPTER 21

"*Amme, mole karayanu,*" *Lakshmi called out* as she gingerly tried to get up from the bed. ("Mom, the baby is crying.") Lakshmi winced in pain, because her stitches hurt, but she tried to hurry, hearing little Anuradha wailing her head off from her small hammock made from a cotton sari and two strong ropes anchored to a hook on the ceiling.

Her mother came running from the kitchen. "Ayyo, kutty ezhunnekkandaa. Caesarian kazhinjitte anje devasam alle aayullu. Thaichathe potti pogum!" ("Oh no, you better not get up. It has only been five days since the cesarean section. You might bust the stitches!")

Lakshmi lay back down on the bed, glad to let her mother lift little Anuradha out of her hammock and try to soothe her to sleep. But the baby shrieked again; she was inconsolable. Looking at her scrawny little grandbaby, Nalini fretted, "Endaa ee kuuty ingane karayane. Veshannittaavo." ("Why is this baby crying so much, could it still be hungry?")

CHAPTER 21

When Lakshmi put Anuradha to her breast again, she eagerly accepted it, but two minutes later, she was bawling. As Nalini took the baby from Lakshmi and rocked her in her little hammock, she said, "Ohhhhh, ohhhh, vaava orangikko, ohhhh, ini kuttikke vella dahanakkedaavo?" ("Humming to the baby, baby go to sleep, humming again, could the baby be having indigestion?") She was worried.

Usually, newborns sleep most of the time, but this little one seemed too distraught to sleep for more than four hours at a stretch. Nalini's instincts told her something was wrong. When at last the baby settled down a little bit, Nalini went to the kitchen to prepare the afternoon meal.

Soon, the silence was broken with the cheerful arrival of Lakshmi's friend Divya. She looked beautiful in her red sari, and there was a new radiance to her. Lakshmi put her finger to her lips, indicating that the baby had just fallen asleep and to speak softly for fear of waking her again. Divya went straight to the little hammock and peered inside. She gently kissed the tiny little feet and came back and sat by Lakshmi's side on the bed.

"Ninde pole thanne slim beautiaa. Nalla eishwaram olla mukhanetto. Perum enikkishtaayi." ("She's going to be a slim beauty like you. She has a beautiful face. I like the name too.") Lakshmi's smile was tinged with the worry that was always at the back of her mind.

Undaunted, Divya continued, "Pinne ore good news unde. Ikkollam college kazhiyumbe ende kalyaanam ane. Chekkande family Thrissoornnaane. Pakshe ayaalude achande joli ivideyaayathe konde ivide thanneyaa veede. M.A kaaran lecturer ane, St. Thomas Collegile. Kaanaan tharakkedilla. Pinne vellia forwardaa. Enne cinemakkokke konde poyi. Achane ishtaavinilla.

Pinne nivirthi illaande sammathichathaa." ("I have some good news to tell you. When I finish college this year, I am going to get married. The boy's family is from Thrissoor. But they are settled here because of his father's job. He has a master's degree and is a lecturer at St. Thomas College. Not too bad to look at. He is a little forward and took me to a movie. My dad did not like it, but then, he had no choice but to agree to it.") They both giggled, and for five minutes, it was like old times. When Divya left, Lakshmi was feeling optimistic again.

Satheeshan and his parents came to his in-laws' house to see his newborn for the first time. Awkwardly he looked towards the bed and asked his wife, "Caesarian kazhinjitte kozhappam onnum illallo?" ("You have no problems after the cesarean, right?") Lakshmi smiled and shook her head to indicate she was fine. He went to the hammock and looked at his little daughter who, for once, was peacefully sleeping.

He turned around and joined his father and father-in-law on the veranda. The men talked about politics, the new left-wing ministry that was supposed to uplift the masses from poverty, and the prevailing general corruption.

Back in Lakshmi's room, the mother-in-law insisted on taking the baby out from her hammock and laid her on Lakshmi's bed.

From her plastic bag with the logo Kalyan Jewellers, she took out two small gold bangles and two little gold anklets, and officially put them on the child. "Endeeshwaraa,ende melinjittaane, ellum tholeem maathram. Kuttikke kodukkaan avyashathine paalille?" ("Dear God, the baby is so thin, all skin and bones. Don't you make enough milk to feed her?")

Little Anuradha chose precisely that moment to set up a big wail as if in protest, and Lakshmi and her mother were put on the defensive. Nalini said, "Oraazhchayalle aayittullu, vayare onne shariyaayi varande. Namakke ummarathe kaappi kudikkam." ("It has only been one week since she was born, the little one's stomach must settle down. Why don't we go to the veranda and drink some coffee?")

She ushered the unconvinced mother-in-law out of Lakshmi's room, leaving her daughter to cope with the crying infant. The mother-in-law gave one last look at the infant, and her calculating eyes rekindled the fires of worry in Nalini and Lakshmi once again.

Around eleven the next morning, Lakshmi's brother, Balan, ran into the house, all excited. "Amme, government collegile admission liste post cheythu. Enikke admission unde. Ende friendsum avideyaa pone!" ("Mom, the admission list for the government college has been posted. I have gotten admission there. Some of my friends are also going there!")

His mother looked relieved. Balan was no great scholar; he had barely scraped through the school final with a pass grade. Some colleges had rejected him; the only one that would accept him was the government college, with its notorious lack of standards in education, its constant student strikes, and its substandard teaching.

Its single claim to fame was that it was generally nondiscriminatory in social class and income. Hence it provided an opportunity for people from lesser socioeconomic backgrounds and scheduled castes (the lower castes in the social hierarchy that are sometimes referred to as the underprivileged classes) to go to college. They even had a designated number of seats set aside for the underprivileged castes.

Being forced to take students of all calibers, these government colleges could never compete academically with the private colleges. The other main attraction for a government college was that the low fees provided accessibility to many. Given his less than stellar academic achievements in school, Balan was grateful for the opportunity to go to any college.

He was already looking ahead. "Amme, enikke pudiya paantum shirtum eduthe tharo. Pudiya stylile vellia collar aayitte? Aa pudiya cinemele Jayan adaa ittekkane." ("Mom, will you get the tailor to stitch me a new pair of pants and shirt in the new style, with the big collar? In the new movie, the actor Jayan is wearing a shirt like that.")

His mother laughed at the young man's audacity. Lakshmi, who had just started to walk around the house after her week of bedrest, heard this and said, "Ee maramandane collegee vittathonde endaa gunam? Fees nashtam athre ollu. Thotte thoppi itte varum." ("What's the point of sending this blockhead to college? You are just going to waste the money given in fees. He is going to fail miserably.")

She had not meant for it to sound so bitter, but years of having to put up with a double standard had infuriated her, and she could not help herself.

Although Balan shrugged it off in typical youthful exuberance, Nalini was incensed. "Aavashyam illathathe paranje dosham undaakkaruthe. Avan padiche paassaayee joli eduthe kudumbam nokkanullathaa. Pinne vayassaavumbo njangaleyokke aare nokkum?" ("Don't talk nonsense and jinx the kid. He has to study, pass the exams, and take care of his own family one day. Besides, when we get old, who is going to look after us?")

To Nalini, this differentiation between men and women and their respective destinies was an accepted part of life, just like giving birth and taking care of the children. But Lakshmi had

CHAPTER 21

seen some from her generation of women enter the workforce in small numbers as teachers, doctors, nurses and in minor administrative jobs. She could not shake off her resentment that quickly.

As she lay in bed in the quiet of the night with little Anuradha by her side, close to the wall so she would not fall out of the bed, the events of the day played in her head. It had not been a good day. Much as Lakshmi tried to be magnanimous about Balan's small achievement, some part of her felt the grievous injustice of it all.

Earlier that day, Divya's visit had seemed, at first, to be purely social. Nalini beamed when she saw Divya. "Lakshmi paranju, kalyaanam anenne. Nalla kaaryam. Saareem aabharanom okke eduthe kazhinjo?" ("Lakshmi told me that you were getting married. That is wonderful news. Have you already purchased the sarees and the ornaments?")

Divya shyly answered, "Sari Fashion Fabricseennaa eduthe, aabharanokke Bheemennum. Avedayaa nalla ponnennaa muthashi parayane. Chekkanum avante achanum ammem koode vannirunnu. Ale ennode varthaanam parayaan nokkindaayirinnu. Muthashikkishtaayilla." ("The sarees were bought at Fashion Fabrics and the ornaments are from Bheema Jewellery. Grandmother is always saying they have the best gold. The boy and his parents also came with us. He was trying to talk to me. My grandmother did not like that.")

Nalini chuckled as she walked towards the kitchen. "Pazhe alkaaralle, athonnum ishtaavilla." ("She is an old lady; she will not like that.")

As soon as Nalini was out of earshot, Divya directed Lakshmi to her bedroom. She obviously had something to tell Lakshmi that she did not want Nalini to hear. Since Divya had come by a few days earlier to see the baby, her sudden return had puzzled

Lakshmi. But she had chalked it up to her friend's excitement about her impending wedding. Sadly, Lakshmi had read her childhood buddy correctly—there was indeed something on Divya's mind.

Divya came right to the point. "Athe, Satheeshane patti chelathokke kekkanunde. Randaazhchakke mumbe njaan ayaale officeenne erangi varana kandu, koode joli cheyyana Jaanakiyum aayitte, velia chireem varthaanom okke aayirunnu. Ayaale enne kandilla. Athe athra sukhaayitte thonneella, pakshe pottenne vichaarichu. Appo rande divasam mumbe, ayaale Jose theatereenne avalude koode cinema kazhinje erangi varanathe ende ettan kandu. Parayaan veshamam unde. Pakshe nee ariyaathirunnitte endaa karyam." ("Listen, I have been hearing a few things about Satheeshan. Two weeks ago, I saw him coming out of his office with his colleague Janaki, and they seemed to be flirting with each other, talking and laughing. Thank God, he did not see me. I did not feel good about it, but I did not want to make a big deal out of it. Then two days ago, my elder brother saw Satheeshan coming out of Jose movie theatre after a midnight show with her. I feel bad telling you about this, but there is no point in hiding the truth from you.")

A chill encircled Lakshmi's heart. She started to cry, afraid for her future and even more afraid for her little Anuradha. These were tears of helplessness, that she was unable to protect her daughter from outside forces.

Later, in the still night, unable to sleep, a silent dread came over Lakshmi, and she put a protective arm over her sleeping infant. She took in the sweet smell of her newborn and hoped that tomorrow would bring better news.

CHAPTER 22

"*Endore karachilaane ee koche!* Ingane kuttiyole karayane kandittilla. Ee veettile chevi kekkaan pattaandaayi. Aa kaniyaare viliche jaathakam onne nokkichaalo?" ("This child cries so much! I have never seen children cry like this. No one can hear anything in this house anymore. Shall we call the astrologer and look at her astrology?")

Shankaran was sitting in his dining room, trying to eat the breakfast of dosa and chutney Nilani had put before him. On the veranda, Lakshmi was walking up and down with little Anuradha, who was wailing her head off. "Hmmmm, hmmm." Lakshmi tried humming to the child to soothe her.

The baby was having difficulty feeding, and Lakshmi felt her milk was slowly drying up from anxiety. She was considering feeding Anuradha with a bottled baby formula to help her gain a few precious pounds on her emaciated body. While these thoughts swirled through Lakshmi's mind, she heard her father's question about calling an astrologer. An uncharacteristic rage came over her.

Striding into the dining room she declared, "Ente kutteede jaathakam aarum nokkandaa. Avalde thalelezhuthe vanne poykolum, kaniyaarude sahaayam illaande. Ende nokki nokki ithre etheele!" ("I don't want anybody to look at my daughter's astrology. Whatever her fate is, it will happen, with or without the help of the astrologer. Look at the state I am in after all the astrology that was consulted for me!")

Suddenly leaning against a wall, she slid down and sat with the baby on the floor, and her tears became torrents.

Her parents were alarmed. Nalini said, "Endaa kuttee indaaye ithine maathram karayaan. Anumolde vayarokke shariyaavum. Korache divassam edukumennalle ulllu. Pinne chelappo pudiya prasavicha pennungalkkokke, ingane okke sangadam varum. Athe ithra kaaryaakkaanonnum illa." ("Dear child, nothing happened here that should make you cry so much. Little Anubaby's stomach will settle down, it will just take a few days. And sometimes, new mothers experience a certain sense of sadness, which is natural. It is nothing to be overly concerned about.")

As Lakshmi's sobs grew louder, her mother took the whimpering baby out of her hands. Her father helped Lakshmi to the bench by the side of the dining table. They knew their daughter well enough to realize that something else was bothering her.

Slowly, in bits and pieces, what Divya had told her came out between bouts of tears. Nalini and Shankaran were nonplussed. That a boy from a decent family whom they had, after much inquiry, married their daughter off to, would engage openly in such cheap and disrespectful behavior was beyond anything they could imagine. And when his wife had just given birth to his child!

CHAPTER 22

They did not want to believe the story. Although in such a small conservative town, a story like this would not be told without some veracity, Lakshmi's parents still hoped fences could be mended, and their daughter could be sent back to her husband to live "happily ever after."

"Athokke aalkkaare oronne paranje indaakane alle. Athilonnum vellia kaaryamilla. Thozhilillande irikkumbo paradooshanam parachilaa hobby," Shankaran said. ("That is just loose talk from some people. You don't have to take that seriously. When people don't have much to do, gossip becomes their hobby.")

Shankaran hoped his upbeat speech did not sound as hollow to his daughter as it did to his own ears. When his wife urged him to finish his breakfast, he pushed the plate away, saying, "Ethra doshayaa ittekkane, vayare neranju. Ini enikke venda." ("You have put so many doshas in my plate that my stomach is full. I can't eat anymore.") He washed his mouth, picked up his bag with his lunch and went to work. He looked preoccupied.

After lunch, the baby finally settled down for an uneasy nap. Lakshmi and Nalani were exhausted from taking turns walking up and down the veranda, soothing Anuradha in their arms. Lakshmi gingerly placed her on the bed so as not to wake her and put two round pillows on either side of her to keep her from rolling over the side. She sat on the bed looking at her sleeping infant for a few minutes before gently kissing her on her brow. The baby reflexively moved her lips. Her mother smiled and went to see if she could help in the kitchen.

Nalini was busy cutting up plantains for the mixed vegetable curry for dinner. She looked up, registered her daughter's disheveled appearance and the dark circles under her eyes, and her nurturing instinct welled up. "Kutty orangiyo? Bhedaayi varunnundennaa thonnane. Endeeshwaraa, kaakkane! Ini ende mole poyi onne kuliche dress maatteette vaa. Kulikkaan vellam choodaakki vechittunde. Mole karanjaa njaan nokkikkolaam." ("Did the baby sleep? I think she is getting better. Dear gods, keep her safe! Now, my sweet girl, have a bath and a change of clothes and come back. I have heated some hot water for you. If the baby cries, I'll take care of her.")

Youth's greatest blessing is its resilience, one bred from unbounded optimism. When the heart is young, it is capable of retaining only the good and the noble—the seamy side of life is forgotten easily. As Lakshmi washed and dried her long hair, her worries seemed to recede for the hour during which she enjoyed the familiar comfort of grooming.

But when she hung her towel on the clothesline outside, she saw a single crow perched insolently on the line. "Po kaakke, shoo, shoo!" ("Go away crow, shoo, shoo!") Lakshmi surprised even herself at the aggression she exhibited in shooing away the lone bird.

The anxiety she'd felt from the events of the preceding days returned and clouded her mind. Her husband's callous infidelity, the baby's constant distress, and now this bad omen. A single crow hanging around is often associated with the rituals that follow the death of a relative. The family places food on a banana leaf and leaves it out for the crows to feast on. This is supposed to appease the spirits of the departed.

When Lakshmi came into the dining room after her bath, running her fingers through her long hair to untangle the knots, Nalini's heart melted. "Mole ippozhum sukhaayitte orangaa. Kutty ivide irunne vallathum kazhikkoo, Avale ippo ezhunnekkum."

CHAPTER 22

("The baby is sleeping peacefully. Why don't you sit here and eat something? She might get up any minute.")

Mother and daughter sat together and ate their lunch. To take their minds off the baby, they talked about Divya's impending nuptials, the qualifications of her groom, and how grand the wedding might be. Lakshmi would miss her dear friend once she was married and had family commitments.

After washing the lunch utensils, Nalini stopped Lakshmi from washing out the mud cooking pots. "Athe nee cheyyandaa. Stitch ittathalle. Njaan cheytholaam. Mole ezhunnettittilla. Raathri muzhuvan orangeettillallo. Onnu poyi kedanne kannadakku." ("You don't need to do that. Your stitches might burst. I can do it. The baby is still sleeping. You have been up all night. Why don't you lie down and try to shut your eyes.")

Lakshmi awoke with a start. It was already three o'clock—half an hour past Anuradha's feeding time. She was surprised that the baby had not woken her with her wailing. She was taking in so little milk yet seemed hungry all the time. And within the past two days, whatever milk went into the baby rapidly exited her body in the form of soiled diapers. Lakshmi picked up her little girl to feed her and saw with horror that the baby was unresponsive. She lay like a thin, raggedy doll, hardly breathing.

Panic rose within Lakshmi. "Amme, Amme, onnodi vanne, mole anangunnilla. Ayyyooo!" ("Mom, Mom, please come quickly, the baby is not moving. Oh no!")

Nalini came running from the kitchen. "Kuttikkende pattee? Endeeshwaraa, rakshikkane!" ("What happened? Dear God, please help us!") She frantically massaged the baby's hands and legs, but little Anuradha seemed too tired to move. Her shallow breathing was barely visible beneath the thin muslin dress she wore, and Lakshmi was sobbing uncontrollably.

Nalini tried to keep down the panic rising within her. Handing the baby to Lakshmi, she hurried to the veranda and called for the neighbor's young son, who was playing in their yard. "Mone, Madhu, neeyonne vegam odippoyi Shankaran chettane officeenne vilichonde vanne. Kuttikke theere sukhallya. Doctorinde aduthe konde ponam. Taxi pidiche vegam varaan para." ("Madhu, son, please go and tell my husband Shankaran to come back immediately from the office. The baby is not at all well. We need to take her to a doctor urgently. Tell him to get a taxi and come back right away.")

The boy left immediately on his bicycle. When Shankaran returned with the taxi, Nalini and Lakshmi were still trying to revive Anuradha. Lakshmi tried to feed her, but the milk drooled down the corners of the baby's mouth, as if it took too much effort to drink it.

One look at the pitiful scene told Shankaran all he needed to know. He felt a cold dread. "Vegam taxee kere. Ippo thanne ponam." ("Get into the taxi quickly. We need to go immediately.")

He hurried his wife, daughter, and the bundled-up baby into the car, and locked the house. Before getting into the car, he called to the neighbor's son: "Madhu, nee onne poyitte Satheeshane vivaram ariyikkanam. Onnum indaayittalla, pakshe kochinde thanthayalle, ariyikkaande pattillallo." ("Madhu, please go and inform Satheeshan about what is happening. Not that anything will come off it, but he is still the baby's father, and has to be made aware of the situation.")

The taxi sped to the clinic of Dr. N.J. Joseph. Some instinct made Shankaran tell the taxi driver: "Onne wait cheyyanam, korache serious aane. Kooduthalom chodikkaruthe." ("Please wait for us, the baby is seriously ill. Please don't ask for more money.")

Somehow, ordinary human beings recognize the tragedies of others—it is in their nature. It is also in their nature to extend themselves beyond the capacity of their limited means to help others. The taxi driver nodded, and he waited.

There was a long queue to see the doctor. But sensing the desperation of the little party with the precious bundle wrapped in swaddling clothes, the people made way for them to see the doctor before they did.

The doctor parted the baby's blankets. Seeing the limp little child held by her mother, he braced for what he had to tell them. He put the stethoscope to her small chest and listened carefully. When he took the scope from his ears, he looked towards Shankaran and said, "Kuttikke bhayangara serious aane, valare dehydrated aane. Heartum valare slow aane. Ivide njangalkkini onnum cheyyaan pattilla. Kozhikkotte medical college ashupathreelekke konde ponathaa nallathe. Vegam thanne venam." ("The baby's case is very serious. She is extremely dehydrated, and her heart rate is very slow. There is nothing we can do for her here. You need to take her to Kozhikode Medical College Hospital, and you need to hurry.")

Everyone waiting outside heard the mother's loud wailing. On cue, they gave way for the group to return to their taxi. Sadly, the taxi did not reach its destination. Along the way, little Anuradha decided that this world was not for her. Her last ride was back to her mother's childhood home. All the neighbors soon filled the little yard to help in small ways, although sometimes just to gawk at the human misery unfolding before their eyes.

It is amazing how similar the sounds of distress are everywhere on this earth. Lakshmi clung to her baby as if she would never let her go. When they took the baby out of her hands to get her ready for the last rites, Lakshmi's anguished cries could even be heard on the street.

When the pitiful little body wrapped in white cloth was carried off by the men to its last resting place, Lakshmi tried to run after her, as if her heart was breaking into pieces, and she too desired the permanent silence of the graveyard.

CHAPTER 23

"Edaa Haneefe, inne Alikkaande biriyani engane indadaa?" ("Hey Hanif, how is Alikka's biriyani today?")

Some of the shift workers were coming in for their usual lunch at Alikka's Kerala Canteen. They sometimes wore pants, but more often were wearing their dhotis and vivid turbans. The food was cheap, the atmosphere chaotic, and they felt right at home. They bantered among themselves, and the waiters knew them by name.

Hanif Mohamed was clearing a table. He looked up and flashed his famous dimpled smile. "Innathe biriyani kalakkeet-tunde. Best! Athinde manam kitteette vellam erakki vannadalle," he said. ("Today's biryani is out of this world. It is the best we have ever made! I know all of you came here after smelling it down the street.")

There was collective laughter as the guys chose a table and took seats in some of the dining room's mismatched plastic chairs. They enjoyed the camaraderie of men displaced from their native surroundings, all of whom were trying to find common ground in their new beginnings. The stories they had left behind were those of sadness and despair, so they chose not to speak of them. It was easier to concentrate, even in less-than-fortunate circumstances, on a mirage of hope that better days would come.

"Neeyennum njangalode ithe thanneyalle parayanathe. Biriyani nannaayi nannaayi ini world famous avo?" ("You tell us this all the time. If the biriyani gets any better, will it become world famous?") This was from Asher, the wisecracker. There was more laughter from the table. Hanif, who had come to clean the table, laughed with them, wiping it down with the wet rag in his hand.

"Athine ningalode enikke nona parayaan patto. Appe pinne nere thanne parayaanne vichaarichu. Appo biriyani edukkaam alle." ("I cannot tell you guys a lie. So I figured I might as well tell you the truth. I guess everyone is going for the biriyani. I will bring it out to you.")

It had been three months since Alikka rescued Hanif at the seashore and brought him to the restaurant. He had worked there ever since. The hours were tough, but the work did not bother Hanif too much. With his buoyant personality, he was fast making friends with the other staff and the regular customers.

The young man had a natural friendliness that appealed to people. He was a popular fixture in the dining room, and Alikka took almost paternal pride in pointing this out to his assistant. "Ee Alikka kore pere kandittollathaa. Avan vere ellavarem pole alla. Ore prathyeka charactaraa. Avane ineem pogaanunde." ("This Alikka has seen a lot of people. He is not like all the others. He is a character, all right. He still has places to go.")

CHAPTER 23

Hanif Mohamed took the group's orders. Like the shifting sands on the Gulf Coast, the fortunes of these migrant workers (they were employed mainly in construction), were constantly changing. From their orders, Hanif could tell who was employed and who had hit rock bottom. When money was running out, you shared food with someone else in the same boat, and when you became penniless, you depended on the mercy of others for a meal. It was a support system they had worked out over the years.

Hanif Mohamed balanced four plates of biryani on his arms. He put them down on the table with his usual showmanship. "Ee Arabi naattile best biriyani, Kerala canteenilethe. Daa irikunnu proprietor Alikka. Ningalangerode nanni paranjaa mathi." ("Here comes the best biryani in all of Arabia, available only in Kerala Canteen. Do you see the proprietor, one Mr. Alikka, sitting over there? You can thank him for this.")

Alikka looked up from the cash register and smiled indulgently. Ever since he had brought the boy to his establishment, the whole place had cheered up a little bit. He had not met too many men or women with the people skills of Hanif Mohamed. With Allah's help, he knew the boy would go far. Alikka was a good judge of who would make it and who would fall by the wayside. It was just a matter of time before this bird would fly the coop, and Alikka, for one, would rejoice in his flight.

"Endaa chekkande ore vedi parachile! Edaa Aseeme, ivan pazhe pusthakam vaangichitte Arabi padikkaan nokkaa. Ini aa Sheikhe vaadaga pidikkaan varumbo, ivane vidaam, ayaalode samaadaanam parayaan." ("The boy certainly can talk! Hey, Aseem, did you know that he bought himself a second handbook and is trying to learn Arabic. Next time my landlord, the Sheikh, makes his grand appearance, I will let Hanif deal with him.")

This brought a new round of whooping and hooting. "Athe, vellia enna companeede chairman aavumbe ee paavangale marakkaruthe ketta. Njangalkokke ore watchmaande joli engilum shariyaakki tharanam ketta. Kalle chomanne mathiyaayi." ("Hey, man, when you become the chairman of a big oil company, please do not forget about us poor folks. At least employ us as watchmen. We are tired of carrying stones at the construction sites.")

They liked the goofy young fellow with his quick smile and friendly ways and had formed an easy backslapping friendship with him.

"Haneefe, korache vellam venadaa." ("Haneef, get me some water to drink.") When the water arrived, the men had settled in to enjoy their food and conversation dwindled. These were men for whom a meal was a luxury, and they savored every minute. Hanif knew enough to leave them alone while they were eating. For many, it was their only satisfying meal of the day.

Hanif wandered into the kitchen, where the chopping, cutting, and other preparations for the nightly dinner were being carried out. Occasionally he would come into the dining room to check on the diners. He was clearing the plates when an expensive car pulled up to the curb.

Alikka's face registered his dislike of the owner of the car. "Hamukke, etheettinde, njammande kazhuthine kathi vekkaan. Ippraavashyom vaadaga koottaanaavo plan." ("The bastard has arrived to cut my throat. I wonder if he is planning to increase my rent this time also.")

Nevertheless, he came out from behind the cash register smiling broadly. One would not detect the slightest trace of hostility when he welcomed his landlord with a hand to his forehead saying, "As-salaam alaykum." ("Peace be upon you.")

The Sheikh curtly returned the greeting. He was about to talk to Alikka when Hanif Mohamed saw him from across the room and called out a cheery greeting in Arabic. "As-salaam alaykum, Sheikh, marhaban, ahlaw!" ("Peace, be upon you, Sheikh. Welcome, hello!")

All the words he had painstakingly learned and practiced had come tumbling out in one sentence. The sheikh frowned at the interruption. Then he looked into the face of a handsome young man with smiling eyes and a cheeky dimpled grin and was intrigued. Hanif saw Alikka explaining about his new employee, and the sheikh kept looking his way. Hanif had run out of his extensive vocabulary in Arabic. For want of something else to say, he jauntily asked the sheikh, "Eating biriyani? Very good!"

To the surprise of Alikka and everyone else, the older man smiled and nodded. The proprietor ceremoniously seated his landlord at his best plastic table after Hanif Mohamed made a show of wiping it down several times. While Alikka supervised Hanif as he plated the biryani, he muttered to himself, "Allah, vaadaga poraande ippo njammale thinne mudippikkaan erangi thirichekkaa." ("God, not content with fleecing me with the rent, now he has decided to eat me out of the house.") But secretly, he was honored that his esteemed landlord had decided to eat in his establishment and try his "world-famous" biryani.

When Hanif put the plate in front of the sheikh, the visitor mimed eating, and asked for a spoon. Alikka was all proprietor then. "Edaa inganeyaa sheikhine biriyani kodukkande,ore spoonum koodi kodukkaande? Nammade maathiri kayyonde thinnaan ayaalke ariyo." ("Hey boy, is this any way to serve the sheikh biryani, without even a spoon? He doesn't know how to eat with his hand, like us.")

Hanif ran to the kitchen and, after much foraging, unearthed one of the few spoons there. He quickly washed it and presented it to the sheikh, who nodded his approval. He muttered a blessing over the food and ate with the spoon.

Everyone in the ragtag dining room was enthralled. They were even more amazed when the sheikh was about to finish his meal, and Hanif Mohamed walked up to him with a steaming cup of tea. He placed it in front of the sheikh with, "Hal aejabak altaem?" ("Did you like the food?") The landlord gave a belly laugh and gave him a 'thumbs up' sign to indicate how much he liked it, and simply said, "Shukraan lak." ("Thank you.")

Before leaving, the sheikh said something to Alikka who vigorously nodded his head as they looked toward Hanif Mohamed. The young man smiled and tried to carry on nonchalantly, but he worried that he had overstepped the bounds of propriety. When things quieted down in the restaurant, Alikka approached him with a "Haneefe ore kaaryam parayaanunde. Nammakke store mureelekke poyitte samsaarikkaam. Oronninum pathe cheviyaa." ("Hanif, I need to tell you something. We can go to the storeroom and talk. Everyone here has ten ears each.") Hanif was preparing himself for a lashing from Alikka's famous caustic tongue.

To his surprise, the old man was beaming. "Ayaalke ninne nannaayitte pidichu. Onde machaande construction companeele crane operator aayi joli vaangiche tharaamenaa parenathe. Avare train cheytholum. Njaan paranju ninakke korache padippokke ollathaanenne. Ithe korache technical joliyaane. Nalla shambalom kittum. Endaayaalum onne poyi nokke. Hamukkinde vaakine enthoram velayindenne kaanaalo. Pattikkalaanengi ninakke thiriche varaalo. Enthaayaalum onne anweshichitte vaa. ("That guy was really impressed with you. He is talking about getting you a job as a crane operator in his cousin's construction company. They will train you for the job. I told him that you have completed some college. This is a technical job, so you will be paid well. Anyway, go and see what it is all about. We will soon learn how much that bastard's word is worth. If it doesn't work out, you can always come back here.")

This was the last thing that Hanif Mohammed was expecting, and he was alarmed. To operate one of those cranes that seem to touch the sky felt like a daunting task. What if he made a mistake and the crane came crashing down? To leave the confines of Alikaa's friendly world and venture into the big unknown foreign city was frightening, and yet, at the same time, exhilarating.

Still, he hesitated. "Enikke ivide ore jeevitham thannathe Alikkayaane. Enikke ivide ellarem nalla ishtaa. Ividanne povaan manasse sammathikanilla." ("You are the one who gave me a life here, Alikka. I like everyone here in this establishment. In my mind I cannot come to terms with the fact of leaving all this behind.")

This brought on one of Alikka's famous temper tantrums. "Njaan oronnine kadaleenne pidichonde varanathe duthedukkaanonnum alla. Ithe canteena, anaadha shaalayalla. Nalla joli kittumba poyi nannaayi paniyeduthe jeevikkaan nokke. Chekkande ore varthaanam.") ("When I save some poor soul stranded on the beach, I am not looking to adopt them. This is a canteen, not an orphanage. When you are offered a good job, take it—and try to better yourself by working hard. You are talking nonsense.")

That was settled, then. In that little world, Alikka was the final authority. And that is how Hanif Mohamed started working for the BHS construction group in Dubai.

CHAPTER 24

Lakshmi *awoke with a start.* It was time to feed the baby. Her blouse was drenched in breast milk. She automatically reached for the little form lying next to her on the bed. She felt nothing, and panic rose in her chest. All around her a seeping blanket of darkness seemed to smother her. She heard her grandmother snoring on the bed above her, as Lakshmi lay on her thin mattress on the floor. The time on the small clock on the table read 1:00 a.m., past time for Anuradha's midnight feed.

It was that precious time when a new mother bonds with her little one, holding her close, yet again giving her life from within herself. She could almost smell the baby—a mixture of talcum powder, coconut oil (used to massage her tiny body), and the familiar scents of digested milk and baby spit. It was almost too much to bear. Lakshmi started to sob, which woke her grandmother.

The old woman gently rocked the broken young woman in her arms and crooned, "Ende kutty karayaandirikku. Ellaam deyva nishchayaanenne koottiyaa mathi. Ippo thonnum sahikkaan pattilyaanne. Korache kazhiyumbo ithum ore vedanayolla ormayaavum. Ammoomma anubhavatheenne parayanathaane." ("My sweet girl, please stop crying. Think of this as God's will. Now it seems like too much to bear. But one day it will recede into a painful memory. Your grandmother is talking from her own experience.")

A few years before Lakshmi's mother was born, the grandmother had lost a newborn to an unknown illness. The baby had been found in her little sari hammock, with vomit from her mother's milk running down the side of her open lips. Although many things had faded from her mind, the old woman still remembered the desperation of that moment with frightening clarity.

The atmosphere in the house did not lift with the dawning of a new day. Ammoomma could be heard telling her daughter in the kitchen, "Nalini, korache kaachiya paalile mathuram itte, aa kuttikke kodukku. Raathri muzhuvanum karachilaayirunnu. Veshamam thetti thetti varaane." ("Nalini, do take some of that newly boiled milk with some sugar to that girl. She was crying all through the night. She is racked with waves and waves of sadness.")

As has happened from time immemorial, the world of women was protecting one of its own. The mother and grandmother coaxed Lakshmi to drink at least a glass of milk. As they painstakingly washed her long hair and dried it with an *eerazhathorthe* (a thin, cheesecloth-like towel), she sat still as a stone. Nalini warmed water on the stove for Lakshmi to bathe her body. Together, the women bound up her breasts with an old cloth to stop her lactation.

Lakshmi's friend Divya dropped by often, and would help her friend dress. Now a newly married woman, Divya would

CHAPTER 24

regale Lakshmi with the happenings in her husband's household. She told her about her new sister-in-law, who was a fashion plate. With elaborate disapproving gestures Divya informed her friend, "Vellia Sheelayaanennaa vichaaram. Blousinde backe bra cover cheyyum, athrem thanne. Ende bhartaavu paranju, nee adonnum kande cheyyandaanne. Enikkum athrem stylonnum ishtallya." ("She thinks she is the movie star Sheela. The back of her blouse just about covers her bra, that's all. My husband told me I better not try to imitate her. I don't like those kinds of extreme styles anyway.")

Divya was working as a schoolteacher, and she had plenty to say about the kids in her class and the other teachers in the school. Even the management was not spared in her running commentary.

At first, the normalcy of Divya's life was a headache for Lakshmi, a definite irritation. But after a few months, she felt herself being slowly drawn back into the world of people. She would still burst out in fresh tears at the thought of the precious life snatched from her, but she was also dealing with the new realities she faced.

When the customary three months after the birth of the baby had elapsed, Lakshmi's parents became alarmed. Traditionally, the husband was supposed to come to his in-laws' home, and with much fanfare, take his wife back to the house they shared. This marked the end of the process of pregnancy and childbirth. From then on, the new mother coped with her infant on her own.

There was no word from Satheeshan or his family about when they would come to get Lakshmi. Shankaran was worried. He talked this over with Nalini privately. They did not dare to mention this to the grandmother in case she blurted out something to Lakshmi, causing her even greater anguish.

One night, Shankaran told Nalini his decision. "Naale njaanonne Satheeshande veede vare poyi varaam. Avarendaa uddeshikkanenne onnariyanallo. Kutty marichitte, athinde karmangalokke kazhinjitte ingatte ethiche nokkeetum koodi illa, avan. Ithendore perumaattam aane. Ore sneham ilyaatha vargam!" ("Tomorrow I will go to Satheeshan's house. We need to know what they are thinking. After the baby died and the funeral formalities took place, he has not been here even once. What kind of behavior is this? They are very cold people!")

When people live in the same household, even without being told, news, especially bad news, has a way of dispersing into the very air. Dimly, Lakshmi was aware of the tension in the house, and she knew the reason for it. Amid her grief, her anxiety grew.

When her father was uncharacteristically late from work the next day, she asked her mother why.

Nalini tried to hide her nagging sense of doom. She reassured her daughter: "Aa athe joli kazhinjappa vella parichayakkaarem kandittindaavum. Appo varthaanam paranje ninnappo samayam poyade arinjittundaavilla." ("He must have run into somebody he knows. They probably got talking, and he lost track of time.")

Knowing her father as she did, Lakshmi realized this was highly unlikely. It was almost eight o'clock when mother and daughter heard the familiar creaking of the garden gate being opened.

As Shankaran walked up the steps to the house, he seemed to have aged ten years. Without a word, he handed his wife his lunch container and umbrella, and sat down heavily in a chair on the veranda. Nalini ran to the kitchen to get him a steaming glass of tea. Lakshmi, seeing her father's mood, disappeared into her room.

CHAPTER 24

Only after Shankaran finished the tea did Nalini dare ask him about his visit to Lakshmi's in-laws. "Endaa indaaye, avarenne varaamenaa parayane? Ee penninde dukham avarke orthe koode." ("What happened, what did they say? It is not beyond them to figure out the grief of this girl.")

Shankaran shook his head and explained. Satheeshan's parents had both been at home, and they were cool towards him. They did not ask him to sit down, and when he tentatively broached the purpose of his visit, they acted extremely cagey. The father looked terribly uncomfortable, but it was the mother who spoke.

"Kalyaanam kazhichappe Chowwadoshaanenne paranjollu. Athe konde maathram ithrem kashtapaadugalonnum varilla. Ningade kuttikke vere chela jyothisha doshangalum koode indaavumenaa njangade kaniyaare parayane. Appo ini Satheeshane vere endokke sahikkandi varum. Pinne avan parayanathe avalke ore sneham illyaatha prakirthi aanennaa. Avande kale moshaayathonde avale avane maanikkanillaannaa avande veshamam. Avanee bandham vendaannaa parayane." ("When the marriage was arranged, we were told only that the girl had the astrological problem of Chowwadosham. But that alone does not explain all the terrible things that happened after the marriage. When we consulted our astrologer, he was of the belief that your daughter has something more wrong in her astrology than what was first believed. If that is the case, God alone knows what other tragedies our Satheeshan would have to face being married to her. Our son told us that she does not have a loving nature at all. He firmly believes that because of his physical handicap she does not give him the respect that is his due as her husband. He does not want to continue in this alliance.")

It took Shankaran a couple of minutes to digest this. When he did, he was beside himself with anger. "Ningalokke nalla kudumbakkaaraayirikkum enne brokere orappe thannittaa kalayaanam nadatheethe. Ithende maryaatha aane? Olla aabharanom, sreedhanom okke thanne, andassaayi ore kuttie kettichayachade ningalke thonnumbe vendaanne vekkaanalla. Njangalum korache kaaryangalokke kekkanunde. Satheeshane aaro koode joli cheyyana pennaayitte lohyaanennum, orumiche cinemakkokke pondennum okke. Ende kutteede sangadam kaanaan ningalkaarkum ore hridayam ille. Avale ingane veshamippichaal eeshwaran porukkilla." ("This marriage took place because the broker assured us that you were from a good family. What kind of behavior is this? I married my girl in good faith, giving the promised ornaments and dowry. You cannot just discard her whenever you feel like it. We are also hearing a few things about your boy—that he is overly friendly with some female at work, and they were seen at the movies together. You don't even have the heart to see my daughter's sorrow. The gods will not forgive you if you hurt a girl like this.")

At that moment, Satheeshan returned from work. One look told him what was happening. When Shankaran tried to confront him about what his mother had said, Satheeshan walked into the house, and Lakshmi's father felt slighted. He could tell that their minds were already made up; there was no use in talking.

But the mother-in-law was not finished. "Ningale kodutha thucha sreedhanathine patti aano parayanathe? Athippo avale avan rande kollam ponne pole nokki koduthille. Athinde kanakokke veetti kazhinju. Pinne aabharanam avalde kayyee thanne ille. Njangalidithittonnum illallo.Pinne ende mone patti angane apavaadam parayanda. Ningade molum endaande muslim

CHAPTER 24

chekkanaayitte ezhuthe kuthe nadatheennokke njangalum kettu. Penninde thalelthe kuruthakkede njangalkke ineem budhimutte indaakanene mumbe, namalkee bandam ozhippikkaam." ("Are you talking about the puny dowry you gave your daughter? He took care of your daughter well for two years, so we are square. Her ornaments are in her possession, anyway. We haven't taken them or anything else. I would advise you not to spread ugly rumors about my son. We have also heard gossip about your daughter exchanging letters with a Muslim boy, or something to that effect. Before we suffer any more tragedies because of your daughter's ill-fated astrology, it is better to end this relationship.")

She said this with finality, and her husband nodded his assent. Shankaran could say or do nothing more to change their minds. Insulted and dejected, he turned and left.

Nalini could not believe her ears. She started to cry. "Endaa ee parayane, kutty marichitte avalonne nadakkaan thodangeettollu. Ippo ithengineyaa sahikkaa." ("What are you saying? She has just started to stand up after the baby died. Now she will have to bear this news too.")

Behind the door, Lakshmi heard every word uttered. She felt like a tomb was closing in on her; she could not breathe. There was no way out.

CHAPTER 25

Lakshmi *cringed in her small room.* It had become her universe, where the failings of her life played over and over in her mind. The beautiful little life she thought she could nurture and thus bring a certain meaning into her existence, was hers no more.

The love that had welled up in her with every little coo and toothless smile dried up. She felt like driftwood—that any current could carry her crashing onto a rock. She cried until the tears came no more for the baby she had loved and lost, the baby who had brought focus and purpose into her life.

As for the marriage, she was relieved that the drama was over, glad to no longer have to deal with the temper tantrums of a man with an inferiority complex and the pervading oppressiveness that hung in the air of their small rented house.

It had not been a relationship of two people building a life together, supporting one another, and living with hope for the future. Lakshmi had lived in constant fear of criticism: how she cooked, or made tea, or even her looks or the way she dressed. Satheeshan's scowl when he first saw her had never left him, nor had his air of grievance. He believed the world owed him something for having to go through life with a physical handicap.

Lakshmi felt somewhat free only when he was at work. But the moment he returned, the air in the house seemed polluted, and the questions would start about her activities that day. He was always suspicious. So the only times she left the house were when he took her to a movie, or they visited his or her parents. He would buy provisions on his way home from work, making sure that Lakshmi did not have to go outside for even this small housewife's pleasure.

She had no money of her own, and in the two years they were married, he had not bought her even one single sari to wear. Once, when she suggested she could visit her parents when he was at work, he acted like she had said something outrageous.

"Nalla veettile pennungale vazhi thendi nadakkaarilla. Avare bharthaakkanmarude koode pogum, athrem thanne. Ithe evidethe sheelaane pennungale vazheele kaalene azhiche vittonam karangi nadakkanathe. Ninde kootte kaarithi Divyem Shailaja teacherokke angane orodethe thaniche ponidenne paranjitte ninde manassile aa moham venda. Nee ivide adangi odungi kazhinjaa mathi." ("Women born in good families don't roam the streets alone. They go with their husbands, and that's all. What kind of behavior is this where women wander through the streets like cows untethered from their posts? I know your friend Divya and Shailaja teacher go alone to take care of errands, but don't entertain any such ideas for yourself. I expect you to live in this house modestly, not bringing too much attention to yourself.")

But now as Lakshmi sat in her room, afraid to go outside and deal with a cruel world, she wondered if she had merely exchanged one prison cell for another.

She noticed a subtle change in the household dynamics. Her father rarely spoke to her. Occasionally, she would catch him looking at her with irritation, as if she was responsible for how things had turned out. She knew that when he married her off, he had heaved a sigh of relief that his duties by her were over, and he did not want to know what was happening in his daughter's household.

It was a woman's duty to adjust to her husband and keep him happy and content. Shankaran wasn't sure if his cerebral daughter had done everything in her power to save her marriage. It is true that he had noticed an irritability and sharpness of tongue in his son-in-law, but he was a man with a responsible job. If he was a little strict with his wife, it was not a bad thing. Sometimes, in Shankaran's opinion, women needed to be handled with discipline.

Lakshmi's mother and grandmother were more sympathetic. Occasionally, Lakshmi even heard her mother sticking up for her in her parents' room. "Ayaale ore moradan manushyanaa. Ore mayom illya. Ore cinemakke koode konde pogaan enthoram kenchanam enne ningalkariyo. Pinne bhaarya ollappe vere penninde pinnaale pona aanungale patti enikke vellia abhipraayam onnum illya!" ("He is a mean-spirited man. Not at all kind. He would not even take her for a movie without the poor girl begging for it. And of course, I do not have much of an opinion about a man who goes after another woman when he still has a wife!")

Lakshmi's father would get irritated and blame Nalini for not bringing up their daughter with proper decorum, so she would

CHAPTER 25

know how to act as a traditional wife. But Lakshmi's adversity had strengthened her mother's backbone. Just when you think you know a person, human beings are so complex, they will surprise you.

Ammoomma was the biggest surprise of all. One night, as Lakshmi sat on her bed with her knees pulled up, a picture of dejection and despair, the old woman was, as usual, going through her rituals before laying her head down for the night. She carefully hung her outer garment on the clothes rack and pulled her scanty hair into a knot on top of her head. Then she sat on her bed, closed her eyes, and put her hands together in prayer. "Naaraayanaa, naaraayanaa" (calling the name of God), she chanted her nightly devotions.

When Ammoomma opened her eyes, she was struck by the overwhelming sadness and utter hopelessness of the form sitting silently on the mattress rolled out on the floor. In her husky voice, the grandmother reassured the desolate young woman, "Kutty orangaan nokke. Ellaathinum eeshwaran ore vazhi indaakkum. Ammoomma nannaayi praarthikkunnunde, ende kuttikke vendi. Ende manasse parayanu ellaam shariyaavumenne. Kutty kedakku." ("Try to get some sleep, sweetheart. God will show us a way out of everything. Your grandmother is praying hard for her sweet child. Somehow, my heart tells me that everything will work out. Lie down and get some rest.")

Even when the divorce papers arrived for Lakshmi to sign, writing away her marriage forever, she was unfazed. When she put her signature to the paper that ended the union, she felt no remorse. A broken relationship could lead to heartache, but where there had been only a tenuous cohabitation, there was nothing to grieve.

The one thing that would change was Lakshmi's place in society. She would have to endure the embarrassment of her parents, and the cruel glances and slashing, whispering tongues when she stepped outside, as if the failure of her marriage could be solely attributed to her. She would be the one mothers would point out to their daughters as a warning of how not to behave. These same mothers would warn their sons about the dangers of marrying independent, strong-willed women.

Happily, her friend Divya was always a source of consolation and encouragement. She came whenever she could, even incurring the displeasure of her mother-in-law, who thought Lakshmi was not someone Divya should be friends with. Her dear friend, now three months pregnant, would come and regale Lakshmi about all the events happening in town.

To the young woman for whom nothing had gone right for two years—ever since her ill-fated marriage—this was a lifeline, one she eagerly grasped. Two months after Lakshmi's divorce, Divya mentioned that she had seen Satheeshan and his new wife exchanging garlands at the temple, in front of their families.

It meant little to Lakshmi, who had closed that chapter in her life, but it made Divya livid with anger, and she could hold her tongue no longer. "Ambalathile ninne vellya iliche maala idanundaayirunnu. Aa pezhacha pennine kaanaan onninum kollila. Avane nannaayi cherum. Kalyaanam kazhinjitte sadka sadkaanne nadanne ponindaayirunnu. Ingane mahaa paapam cheyyanorkaa deyvam ingane oro shaapam kodukkaa." ("He was standing at the temple with an idiotic smile, garlanding his new wife in marriage. That loose woman does not look good at all. They are a perfect match for each other. After the marriage, I saw him limping away with his brand-new wife. Only to those

CHAPTER 25

who commit such great sins does God give such debilitating infirmities!")

Divya was hoping to cheer her friend up, but Lakshmi started to cry. "Appo njaanendoram mahaa paapiyaayirikkanam, ende kuttie thanne deyvam eduthonde poyille." ("Then I must be such a terrible sinner, because God thought it was a just punishment for me that he took away my daughter!")

✺

Six months later, Lakshmi's emotions still teetered from grief to despair, with no end in sight. Then one day, as she and her mother were cutting vegetables for the afternoon meal in the kitchen, a woman called out from the veranda: "Ivide aarum ille?" ("Is anyone home?")

When Nalini cautiously opened the front door, there stood Shailaja teacher from Lakshmi's school days, a little older, but with the same kind smile.

"Njaanithile povaayirunnu. Appo Lakshmiye onne kanditte pogaamenne vichaarichu. Kuttikke kore budhimuttokke undaayeenne kettu. Njaanonne avalode samsaarichotte?" ("I was going through this way, and I thought I would visit Lakshmi. I know she had many difficulties. Is it okay if I talk to her?")

Lakshmi came out tentatively, bearing the shame of her situation, but her old teacher's reaction at seeing her put her at ease. "Endaa kutty onnum kazhikkaarille, ingane melinge irikkane. Deham nannaayi nokkanam. Pinne ore sahaayam chothikkaan koodiyaa vannathe." ("What is this girl, don't you eat anything? You have become so thin. You need to look after yourself well. I came here also to ask for your help.")

Shailaja teacher explained that she had retired a year before and was now giving private tutoring sessions in math at her house. She used her veranda and the little lean-to shed by the side of her house as classrooms. Being a skillful teacher, her pupils were doing well, and their numbers had grown exponentially. She was looking for someone to teach the early evening and weekend classes for younger students.

Lakshmi had lost a great deal of confidence and was unsure, but her mother surprised her by jumping in and saying, "Teachere chodikkumbe cheyyaan avalke sandoshalle ullu. Eppazhaa varandenne paranjaa mathi, avale varum." ("Teacher, you know she will be only too happy to do what you want her to do. You just tell her when to come, and she will be there.")

Lakshmi was taken aback at her mother's boldness. But before she could object, Shailaja teacher sealed the deal by saying, "Oro kuttikkum 20 rupa veche tharaan pattum, ore classile ore 6 kuttiyolundaavum, appo korache varumaanom undaavulo." ("For each student I can pay ₹20, and there will probably be six kids in each class. So, you can make a little bit of money this way.")

The death of her baby and the breakup of her marriage had left Lakshmi hesitant; she faced the future with anxiety. Now, for the first time in many months, she felt a sense of awakening, an excitement coursing through her veins.

That evening, when her father heard the news, he was once again irritated. "Indaaya cheetha pere poraandaa ini porathekke poyi aalkaare konde oronne parayippikkaan. Ivide veettile adangi odungi kazhinjaa pore?" ("Are you not satisfied with the bad name you have already brought upon yourself? Now you want to go outside and teach? Isn't it enough for you to live modestly in your own house?")

Lakshmi saw her dreams crumbling, but for once her mother spoke up, exhibiting a temper directed at her father Lakshmi had never seen.

CHAPTER 25

"Identhaa patteem poochem onnum alla veettee ketti idaan. Ore jeevida kaalam muzhuvan avalende cheyyumennaa ningale vichaarichekkane. Avale padippikkaan pononde ore thettum varilla." ("She is not a dog or a cat to keep tied up in the house. What did you think she was going to do for a lifetime? Nothing will happen if she teaches a few classes.") With that, Naliniamma prevailed, for the first time in her life.

On the first day of her new job, Lakshmi dressed carefully, if a bit severely, and braided her hair meticulously. As she came out of her room, Nalini said, "Korache nalla neramulla sari udukkaayirunnille. Ellaavarum kaananathalle." ("You should wear a more colourful sari. After all, you will be seen by everybody.")

Her daughter curtly replied, "Njaan ponathe padippikkaan aane, sowndarya malsarathinonnum alla!" ("I am going to teach in a classroom, not for a beauty contest!")

Her Ammoomma hovered around, urging her to eat one more *vada* (fried lentil donut) with her tea, then gave her two-cents worth of advice. "Mole ore vada koodi kazhikkoo. Deham korache nannaavatte. Pinne aa kuttiole nannaayi adiche padippikkanam, ennaale vellathum athungalude mara thalele kerollu." ("Eat one more vada, sweetie. You need to get a little stronger. Make sure you give those kids a couple of beatings, otherwise nothing will go into their blockheads.")

Lakshmi had to laugh at this. She told her grandmother that one was no longer allowed to beat kids mercilessly because they had trouble at their lessons, unlike in her days. The old woman sighed and replied that the lack of corporal punishment and discipline was the reason for all the ills of the modern generation.

When Lakshmi left the house, grasping her books nervously to her chest, her mother and grandmother walked with her till the outside gate. "Kutty dhairyaayitte poyi vaa. Ellaam nannaavum." ("Be brave and go on. Everything will work out.") With these words they blessed her and sent her on her way.

The two women, who had never stepped foot outside their homes except to go to the temple, and always accompanied by a male, stood outside the gate. They watched the proud, beautiful young woman's receding figure until she turned a bend in the road, and they could see her no more.

CHAPTER 26

When *the silver Jeep pulled up* to the front of Kerala Canteen in the early '70s, all eyes automatically turned towards it. The door opened and the occupant stepped out.

When Alikka saw who it was, his smile lit up his whole face, and the craggy lines seemed to disappear. "Alla, ithaaraa vannekkane? Njaan vella saayippaayirikkumenne karuthi. Nalla nerolla shirtum, paantum, shoesokke itte vella vellakkaare touristekale aayirikkumenne vichaarichu. Vaa vaa, edaa Yousefe, saarekke ore biriyaani edukke. Koode ore chaayem." ("Who is this who has come? I thought you were a European, wearing that colourful shirt with your plaid pants and those fancy shoes. I was sure it must be some tourist. Come, come, hey Yousef, bring the Sir some biriyani and a cup of tea with it.")

The old man felt great pride looking at his young protégé, who had all the trappings of someone who had arrived. With his aviator Ray-Ban sunglasses, his colourful terylene shirt, and shining shoes, Hanif Mohamed looked like a movie star.

He had the easy gait of a man who had made something of himself by his own grit and hard work, not to mention personal charm. He had worked in the hot Arabian sun in makeshift accommodations and had become inured to the eternal discrimination that was part of the lives of all those who came from countries less fortunate than the Gulf—like India, Pakistan, Bangladesh, Yemen, and so on.

But while most ended up precisely where they first started, the abundant hope and youthful optimism of the young man, along with his few years of education (since most of the workers who took construction jobs in the Middle East were either illiterate, or had only some elementary education) gave him opportunities that set him on a different trajectory. His easy camaraderie with those who worked under him, his differential, but friendly attitude towards his superiors, and his willingness to learn new areas of the business, set him apart from all the others.

Hanif Mohamed's natural charm was his greatest asset. Growing up without his mother, he had learned to take care of himself at a young age and realized that more could be accomplished in life with a smile than with an attitude. It was something he never forgot.

To Alikka, Hanif might as well have been the son he never had. Although his wife, Amina, back in Kerala had given him four daughters, they had not been blessed with a male child to look after them in their old age.

"Vandi kanditte puthiya promotion kitteenne thonnenu. Avadethe ettom vellia bossaayo?" ("Looking at that vehicle, I am assuming you got a good promotion. Have you become the big boss yet?")

CHAPTER 26

Hanif Mohamed laughed at Alikka's belief in his capability to succeed. He replied, "Aaay, big boss onnum aayittilla. Ore promotion kitti. Ippo construction site foremaan aane. Companeede vandi aane." ("Oh no, I have not become the big boss or anything like that. I got one more promotion, and now I am the site foreman. This is a company vehicle.")

Alikka proudly introduced Hanif to all the customers: "Nnammade chekkanaane, ivide mesha thodache nadannathaa. Ippo kandille, vellia kaarile varanathe. Kozhappamillaande adwaanichaa ellaarkum inganeyokke aavaam." ("This is our boy. Just yesterday he was wiping tables here. As you can see, he has now come in a big car. If all of you work hard, without problems, you, too, can achieve all this.")

When the biryani came, he directed the waiter to put it down at a table away from the rest of the customers. He wanted to talk to Hanif in private about the young man Raju, who had served him his food. Could Hanif fix him up with a job at the construction site? "Baakkiyolla chekkammaarude pole alla. BA vare padippunde. Joli cheyyaan madiyilla. Pattiengi vellathum shariyaakki kodukkanam." ("He is not like the other boys here. He has a BA degree and is willing to work at anything. If it is not too much trouble, I would appreciate it if you could find him something.") Hanif Mohamed told his mentor not to worry, and to send the young man to the construction site. "Let me see what I can do."

Alikka knew Hanif was as good as his word. He saw a lot of himself in Hanif Mohamed, in that Hanif was always willing to give someone else a break, just as Alikka had given him a break when he desperately needed one, six years earlier. Some people are quick to forget that, while others remember it all their lives.

Hanif started eating, and Alikka was gratified to see the enjoyment on the young man's face. Hanif said, "Ee Alikkaande biriyani, ivide oredathum ee taste kittilla. Thinne kazhinje aa devassam muzhuvanum vaarithinna kayyile nalla manam undaavum. Best!" ("The taste of this biriyani, you will get nowhere else. After you eat it, the smell will never leave the hand you ate with, all through the day. It is the best!")

Alikka beamed with pride, like a father whose child has been praised. "Athine avanmarokke daaldem, masaalede thuttum okke itte indaakanathalle. Ivide nalla neyyum, Keralenne varuthikkana karimasaalem kondaane indaakanathe. Athinde vyathyaasam indaaville." ("All the others make their biryani with vegetable shortening and bits of spices. We make ours with clarified butter and whole spices imported from Kerala. There has to be a difference.")

Hanif Mohamed shook his head in agreement, while he continued to help himself to the biryani with a young man's ravenous appetite.

Alikka enquired about Hanif's father in Kerala. Hanif said his old man still insisted on going to his butcher shop. "Vellia veedokke panithe koduthu ellaa sowgaryangalum aayi. Pakshe Vaappaakke aa vettukathi kayyiliduthaale orakkam varullu." ("I built him a big house with all the modern conveniences, but what's the use? He has to take up the cleaver in his hand every day so he can sleep soundly at night.")

He also told his mentor that he was trying to educate his stepbrothers, and maybe one day bring them over to the Gulf—if they were so inclined. Alikka was impressed by the young man's single-minded determination to forge ahead, and even better the lot of his entire family.

CHAPTER 26

Hanif Mohamed sensed that there was one more thing the old man was waiting for a chance to bring up. He knew Alikka well, and he was not wrong.

Alikka took a deep breath and tentatively started, "Korache naalaayi ninnode ore kaaryam parayaan irikkayaayirunnu. Ivide ninde vaapaade sthaanam enikkaane. Nee ivide vannitte ore aarezhe kollaayille. Nalla joli aayi, nalla shambalam, quarterse, care, bhaaryenem kondaraam. Ende mone naattee poyaa nalla poo polathe pennine kittoole. Nee ore kudumbaayitte santhoshaayitte jeevikkanathe kaanaanolla aagraham konde parenathaa. Alikkande ee therakke kaaranam ummaane konde varaan pattaathathinde dukhande. Ninakkengilum aa bhagyam indaavanam. Ende mon naattee poyitte nikaahe kazhichitte vaa." ("I have been meaning to talk to you about something for some time. It has been more than six years since you came here. You have a good job, salary, and living quarters, a car, and a visa to bring your wife. My dear son, if you go back home, you will get a girl as beautiful as a flower. I want to see you living happily with a family of your own; that is why I am broaching this subject. With my work schedule, I could never bring my wife over, and I have always felt sad about it. I hope at least you will get to enjoy domestic life. Son, why don't you go home and do a Nikkah (wedding).")

Hanif Mohamed laughed and replied, "All in good time, Alikka. There are a few projects here that need to be completed. Then there is a business I am involved in back at home. Let's see how some of these things work out. Then it will be time for me to visit my homeland."

As usual, when he offered to pay for his food, Alikka was so indignant that Hanif put the notes back in his pocket. But he still had to endure Alikka's tirade: "Nee vellia aalaayeenne veche, ithe ippazhum ninde veedaa. Ivide varumbo ore biriyaani tharaanolla vagayokke ee Alikkane Padachon thannittinde. Maryaadakke enne deshyam pidippikkaande poyko. Pinne aa chekkande joleede kaaryam marakkandaa." ("You might have become a big shot, but this is still your house. Whenever you come here, I can still afford to give you a biryani, thanks to Allah. You better leave, before you make me really mad. And by the way, don't forget about that young man I told you about who needs a job.")

A few jaunty steps, a quick wave, and the jeep pulled away from the curb with a flourish and joined the traffic along the main thoroughfare.

CHAPTER 27

Lakshmi *hugged her books and walked faster.* The best part of the day for her was when she was teaching in the small classroom. She was a born teacher. Helping students who faced challenges mastering mathematics and trying to improve their situations came naturally. She put up with no nonsense, but she was also extremely kind and patient. While Shylaja teacher dealt with grades nine and ten, Lakshmi mainly taught the sixth, seventh, and eighth grade kids, with ages ranging from ten to thirteen. Their childish pranks amused her and broke up the repetitiveness of the sessions. Each of them faced academic challenges. Lakshmi became aware that, beyond all else, this was the stigma she had to help them overcome.

She approached math in a lighthearted manner; she did not want to intimidate the pupils by making the task seem enormous. She tried to impart to them the mental outlook that had made math so easy for her. She didn't want them to freeze when they first saw a math problem. She showed them the logic behind the numbers.

The young teacher became popular among her students. They started to look forward to their tutoring sessions, an activity usually deemed worse than being punished! In return, Lakshmi was building confidence in her limited success, a confidence she desperately needed after her recent tribulations.

With assured strides, she walked up to the lean-to shed by the side of Shailaja teacher's house, nodding to Shailaja teacher attending to her students on the veranda. Entering the makeshift classroom, she greeted her pupils with a smile.

But looking over their numbers, she realized that Radhika, the student with the most problems, was absent. "Inne Raadhikakkende patti? Avale vannillallo. Vellorkkum ariyo?" ("What happened to Radhika? She has not come yet. Does anyone know?")

The students glanced at each other uncomfortably. Lakshmi felt a knot in her stomach; she could tell there was more to the story. She had grown fond of the little girl with the sad eyes who sat at the back of the class staring at her books with an air of defeat.

In her first week of teaching, when Lakshmi put a question to Radhika, the girl cowered, and the whole class laughed. Radhika started to cry, and Lakshmi was alarmed.

"Kutti karayanda aavashyam onnum illa. Math budhimutte aayathondalle ellaavarum tuitione varanathe. Namakke step step-paayitte ee kanakke cheyyaam. Appo valare eluppamaavum." ("There is no need for you to cry, child. It is because math is difficult that all of you are here. Let us go step-by-step and try to solve this problem. Then it will become easier.")

With that reassurance she broke down the problem for them. It was evident that they had never been taught like that. Lakshmi was rewarded by a smile on the face of her young pupil. From that day on, there was a special bond between the teacher who had not been dealt the best cards in life, and the pupil whose young life had its own share of challenges.

Lakshmi learned that Radhika came from a family where both parents had only a middle school education, and the father worked as a daily laborer. They wanted their little girl to do better than they had, but their idea of how to "help" her improve her abysmal academic achievement was to beat her in order to make her study harder and improve. This had the opposite effect: the child so dreaded school that she failed a grade. That is when they decided to have her tutored, despite how much they had to sacrifice to pay the fee. That's why Lakshmi felt that this was not a normal absence.

As usual, when her tutoring session ended and the kids noisily departed, she went up to the veranda to talk to Shailaja teacher. "Inne aa Raadhika vanilla. Veettile vella prashnam undaavo avo. Teacherine vellathum ariyo?" ("Today that girl Radhika did not come. I wonder if there are any problems at home. Do you know anything about it, teacher?")

Shailaja teacher hesitated for a moment before making up her mind. She could not protect Lakshmi from every situation in life. She told her the truth.

"Innale kutty poyikkazhinje avalude achan enne kaanaan vannirunnu. 'Kettyon upeshicha pennaane, nalla swabhaava dosham undaavum, teachereke vere aarem kitteele padippikkaan? Enikke ende kuttie aa claassee kaashe koduthe vidaan pattilla.' Inganeyokke paranjitte ayaale poyi." ("Yesterday, after you left, her father came to see me. 'Isn't she the one whose husband left her? She could not be of good character. Weren't you able to find anybody else to teach here? I don't feel like paying good money to send my child to a class like that.' He said all these things and walked out.")

Suddenly, Lakshmi felt small. The tenuous confidence she was starting to gain was in danger of dissipating. Shailaja teacher sensed this, and that Lakshmi was likely considering resigning so as not to bring unnecessary attention to herself or cause the tutoring center any harm.

Softly, the older woman reassured the aspiring young teacher. "Aalukale palathum parayum. Nammalathe kaaryaakki edukkandaa. Jeevikkaan korache tholikkatti okke venam. Njaan kalyaanam kazhikkaathathine patti endokke paranje parathiyathaa. Enikke kudumbathe nokkaanundaayirunnu. Rogiyaaya achane shushrooshikkaan kore kaashinde aavashyam undaayirunnu. Appo kalyaanathine paisem illya, samayom illa. Pinne avarokke poyi kazhinjappo vayassum kore aayi. Pakshe ee paradooshanam parayanore adokke alochikkunnundo? Jeevithathile kuttikke vendathe ingane kekkandi varum. Kettillaanne nadiche mumbokke poyaa mathi." ("People say a lot of things. We don't need to take that seriously. You need a thick skin to live in this world. Because I am not married, people were spreading such rumors. I had to look after my family. My father was an invalid, and we needed a lot of money for his care. There was no money or time left after that for my wedding. And by the time they were gone, I was too old. But all these people who gossip about others, do they think about all this? In your life you will have to bear this kind of gossip a lot. Just pretend you did not hear it and get on with it.")

CHAPTER 27

Lakshmi knew that Shailaja teacher's advice came from bitter personal experience. Yet despite all of Shailaja teacher's life experiences and achievements, Lakshmi's father called the older woman's life "wasted," just because she had not married and had children. It did not matter that she had guided so many young minds to success. This strengthened Lakshmi's resolve not to be beaten down again by malicious gossip.

※

It was not only Lakshmi who reveled in her newfound status as a teacher. Her mother and grandmother waited for her return to hear the stories about the goings-on in her classroom. This was their connection with the outside world.

When Lakshmi told how Radhika's parents beat her because she could not get better grades, the opinion of "The Council" was divided. Nalini felt bad for the little girl and exclaimed, "Inganem hridayam illaatha aalkaare undo. Avarude molke avarude budhi alle undaavullu!" ("What heartless people. She can only have the brains she inherited from these people!")

But Ammoomma, who had grown up in colonial India, with its abject poverty and strict patriarchy, had another take on the situation. "Korache nalla adi kittiyaale kutiiole sradhikollu. Teachermare korache pediyokke venam ee thaanthonnikalke." ("These kids need a few beatings so they will pay attention. It is better that these good-for-nothings fear their teachers a little bit.")

Lakshmi, the third generation, was trying to work out the latest thinking in education now that it was the 1970s. This was to be more mindful about the needs of the child. Corporal punishment was still the general order of the day, but the younger teachers tried to mete this out sparingly, along with more empathetic counseling.

Lakshmi enjoyed her new role as a part-time working woman and reveled in the admiration of her mother and grandmother. Even her father seemed to come around a bit. She thought he was starting to take her seriously when he consulted her before changing his bank—because another bank was giving a new deal called "fixed deposits," which would fetch a much better interest rate, although one had to wait a longer time for it to mature.

The nights were still the hardest to get through. Lakshmi fiercely missed the little bundle that had lain next to her, so dependent on her. To think that she would never again in this lifetime see that beautiful face, or see Anuradha grow up, was a hurt that would never heal.

Divya brought around her baby for them to see. At first Lakshmi felt a choke in her throat, but the little thing, with her round eyes and sweet smile, soon won them all over. Lakshmi and her mother found themselves cooing over the little one and vying with each other to carry her.

"Amme aa ruske ingotte eduthe, kuttikke thinnaan" ("Mom, just get me some rusk so that the baby can eat it.") They all laughed together as the baby gummed it down. "Kothichi, ammede pole thanne. Vetti mizhunganathe kando. Ninde face aane," Lakshmi pronounced. ("A little greedy pig, just like her mother. Look at how she is gulping it down. I think she looks like you.")

Life followed a familiar pattern of housework, tutoring, and an occasional trip to the temple. One evening after work, as her father sat on the veranda sipping his hot tea, he wanted to discuss something with the women.

As he left work, he had run into the broker Narayankutty, who broached a proposal for Lakshmi. "Aale Gulfilaane. Nalla udyogom shambalom okke inde. Pinne veedum, bhaaryene kondu pogaam. Ayaalde aadyathe bhaarya canceraayitte muppathe vayasile mariche poyi. Ayaalke muppathiyezhe vayassaane. Pinne rande kuttiyolunde, anchum ezhum vayasullathe. Avare nokkaan arengilum vende. Appo ayaale kalyaanam kazhikkaan theerumaanichu. Nalla Kaaryaa." ("He is from the Gulf. He has a good job that pays well. He also has living quarters, and he can take his wife over there. This man's wife died of cancer at the age of thirty. He is thirty-seven years old. He also has two children, who are five and seven years old. He needs somebody to take care of them. That is why he has decided to marry. This is a good thing.")

Her father was shocked and angry at Lakshmi's reaction. She fumed, "I am not interested in playing nanny to somebody else's children. I don't want to hear about any more of these stupid proposals! I have no problem being unmarried. It is not a crime against humanity." Shankaran ranted that she was passing up a great opportunity to live what he called "a normal family life" with the protection of a man who could guide her.

In frustration he spat out, "Aa Shailaja teacherinde maathiri onangi irunno. Ore kaalathe ee theerumaanam alochiche dukhikkendi varum.") ("You can stay dried up like that Shailaja teacher. You will regret this decision one day.")

Lakshmi was furious that despite everything Shailaja teacher had done for her and others, her father should still hold the woman in such scorn. Before she could say something that she would regret, she left the veranda.

Nalini tried to reason with Shankaran. "Mole marichitte korache naalalle aayittullu. Pinne aa mahaapaapi avale ittitte poyille. Ippo avalke kalyaanathinem kuttikalem patti onnum chindikkaanolla manasthithiyalla. Ee rande maasathilaa onne korachengilum pazhaya pole aayathe." ("It has been only a short time since the baby's death and the divorce. Give her a little time to think about marriage and kids again. She has only started to become her usual self in the last couple of months.")

Shankaran got up from his easy chair in a huff. Before going off for his bath, he had these ominous words to say: "Avalirunne samayam pole alochikkatte. Arupathe vayassaagumbo, aalkaare chendem kotti vanne kalyaanam kazhichonde poykolum." ("Yeah, let her take her sweet time and think about it. When she is sixty years of age, I am sure people will come with the accompaniment of drums to marry her.")

Hearing these words, Nalini felt anxious.

❀

Lakshmi was trying to explain the intricacies of geometry. "In a right-angled triangle, if one of the other angles is 35 degrees, how much would the third one be?" While she was giving them time to work out the problem before intervening, she happened to look outside. A neatly dressed young woman was talking to Shailaja teacher near the veranda.

As Lakshmi finished her classes, she saw that the woman had left, and Shailaja teacher was about to step into her home. But seeing Lakshmi, she smiled warmly and asked her how things were coming along.

"Aa vanna kutty ende ore studentaa. Veettile kore veshamangalokke undaayirunnu. Avasaanam ammede olla korache aabharanam panayam vechittum, kadam eduthittokke, padichu. Ippo teacheraayitte joli nokkaane, govt schoolile. Enikke kandappo vellia santhoshaayi.") ("That lady you just saw is a former student of mine. She had a lot of financial problems at home. In the end, they sold whatever little jewellry her mother had and

CHAPTER 27

borrowed the rest to send her to college. Now she is a teacher working in the government school. I was so happy to see her.")

Lakshmi walked home with her brow furrowed in concentration. On this walk, she made the first momentous decision of her life. She knew she would face heavy opposition, but she was determined to move ahead. It was frightening, yet she felt exhilarated. Until now, every major decision had been made for her.

Her mother and grandmother were still trying to digest her news when her father returned from work—and hit the roof. "Endaa ivide ellaarkum braanthe pidicho. Aage olla pandam muzhuvan baankeenneduthe panayam vechitte B.A., B.Ed.ine pogaanaa plaan? Ennitte Shailaja teacherinde pole thaniche jeevikkaam. Endokke vidyatharangale kekkanam." ("Has everyone gone mad? You want to take your jewellry out of the bank locker and pawn it to pay for tuition for a B.A., B.Ed. degree. Is that the plan? And you can end up like Shailaja teacher, all alone.")

She was ready for the onslaught. Try as they might, Lakshmi did not back down. She had found her avocation and a way out of her miserable situation, and she was not going to give up on that glimmer of hope. The household was in turmoil for a week, and her father would not speak to her. Her mother and grandmother tried to reason with her that she could still redeem herself through marriage, even a compromised one, but Lakshmi would hear none of it. In the end, the wall of resistance started to slowly crumble, a few cracks at a time.

Ammoomma was the one who verbalized the resignation of the family. "Aa kutteede ennum indaayirunna ore moham alle. Jeevithathile kore aagrahangalokke nadakkaande poyathalle. Ithengilum nadakkatte." ("This is what she has always wanted.

In her life she has had to abandon a lot of her hopes and desires. At least let this wish happen for her.")

In the end, Lakshmi got her way. On the first day of class as Lakshmi climbed into the city bus to go to college, she remembered her grandmother's advice. "Mole sookshiche ponam bussilokke. Aalkaarekkonde onnum parayippikkaruthe." ("You need to be careful when you go on the city bus. Don't give the people an opportunity to gossip about you.")

CHAPTER 28

The little town was alive with excitement. A new multistory movie theatre was being built in the marketplace. From the moment the first metal girders went up, it was the talk of the town. It would be the first air-conditioned movie theatre anywhere in the area. Young and old alike could not wait for it to open.

With its imposing three-level glass façade and its name, "Sapna Theatre" ("Dream Theatre"), emblazoned at the highest point of the glass front, it was by far the most impressive building in the region.

As its name indicated, it was the stuff of dreams. People strolling up and down during their daily activities stopped to stare with open mouths at the bold impertinence of the structure being erected.

Sapna Theatre was on everyone's lips, whether in family homes over dinner, at the local tea stalls where laborers stopped for tea and a banana fry, and even in drunken arguments at Kalyaani's Kallu Shop (Kalyaani's Toddy Shop).

"Njaan kettathe gulfile ore paisakkaaran panam modakki thodangiyathaanennaa. Arabi ponnalle, thelangum!" ("What I heard is that some wealthy person from the Gulf spent first-class Arabian gold to build it. It will have a shine all of its own!") No sooner had the laborer Raaghavan made this grand statement than another worker, Chakkochan, jumped up, jabbing with his finger: "Athokke konde kala, ithe Fashion Fabricsekaare panitha theateraa. Ore vivaram illaande kedanne koogaa. Nee podaa." ("Just drop all that nonsense. The owners of Fashion Fabrics are building this theatre. You have no idea, and you are talking nonsense. Get lost.")

On top of all of Toddy Shop's alcohol fumes, this was enough to ignite a skirmish between the two esteemed gentlemen. Only when the brazen owner of the establishment, Miss Kalyaani herself, stepped in and gave them a piece of her mind, did they return to their respective benches to sip their toddies in a sullen stupor.

"Athinde odamasthanmaare aaraayaalum athe paranje ividathe koojem glassum onnum thalli pottikkaan njaan sammadikkilla," Kalyaani had proclaimed. ("I don't care who owns the theatre, I will not let you guys break my jars and glasses arguing about it.")

In unison, the men chorused: "Thumba poo nirammulla, thaamarappoo kanulla, Kalyaani neeyende karalalle!" ("With your skin like a beautiful white flower petal, and your eyes like a lotus flower, Kalyaani, you are the queen of my heart!") This was a daily ritual, and even the tough lady proprietor was smiling.

❁

Lakshmi, her parents, and Ammoomma were eating dinner. It had been a year since Lakshmi had graduated from the teacher training program. Her parents and others around her noticed a marked difference in the tentative, unsure young girl. At twenty-four, she had blossomed into a young woman with poise, confidence, and determination.

Her decision had radically changed the course of her life, from being dependent to attaining a degree of independence. After just a couple of interviews, she was hired as a math teacher at the local government high school. This proved convenient because she could walk to work from home. Every morning her mother and grandmother fussed over her lunch. They would even wait at the gate, watching her receding figure. Every evening she returned with stories of kids who were misbehaving, parents who lacked motivation, and the gossip among the teachers.

One day, Lakshmi came back particularly incensed, because the other female teachers were trying to make a matrimonial match for her. "Ellaathindem vaayele naakke pathe mailolam varum. Aa paavam commerce padippikkana saarinode chodikkaa, pudiya Lakshmi teachere ishtaanonne. Ayaalende parayaanaa. Chirichu, appo avare vitte kodukkande. Pinnem pinnem chodikkanu. Appo njaan paranju, enikke ee janmathile ini kalyaanam vendaanne." ("Their tongues are ten miles long. That poor commerce teacher. They kept asking him if he liked me. What is he to say? He just smiled, yet they would not let him be. I piped up and told them that I did not plan to get married in this lifetime.")

Her parents were alarmed, and her mother and grandmother chided her for making such impetuous statements. Of course, Shankaran had never approved of girls going to work. According to him, they become too independent. After that, they never listen to their parents or husbands and make their own decisions.

When Lakshmi got her first paycheck, she brought home a sari for her mother, a dhoti with a thin gold border for her grandmother, and shirt material for her father. The women were excited, but Shankaran did not approve. Women going by themselves to stores, and spending money on whatever they chose! He was sure this marked the downfall of the family structure as he knew it. Not only did men of his generation talk about this all the time, but "working women wearing the pants in the house" was spoofed often in the cinemas.

The consensus of the men of Shankaran's generation was that such independence made women bossy. They failed to get the permission of their fathers or husbands before acting on their whims, thus bringing ruin on the family. "Korache kaashe vannapozhekkum, thala veerthitte, ade muzhuvanum thonniyathile konde chelavaakkikko. Aarodum chodikkem parayem onnum vendallo." ("When a little money comes in, it gives the person a swollen head. Go ahead—spend it all on whatever you like. Of course, you don't have to ask anybody.")

This put a damper on an otherwise festive mood. Shankaran was even more irritated when his otherwise docile wife dared to speak up. "Avalude ore sandosham, athre alle ullu, ningalingane pirupirukkaanonnum indaayilla." ("These are just tokens of her happiness, that is all. There is no need for you to grumble so much.") Although at first Shankaran did not get the shirt material stitched, Lakshmi insisted, and finally he gave in.

A few weeks later, as Lakshmi got up to wash her hands after dinner, a hired car hoisting banners about the new theatre opening passed by. A huge loudspeaker atop the car announced the grand opening on Friday, in time for the weekend crowds.

"Ellaavarum variga, ningalellaavarum kaathirunna pudiya Sapana air-conditioned theaterinde ulghaadanam Trichur jilla collector M. Krishnamoorthi avargal velliaazhcha krithyam naale

CHAPTER 28

muppathine nirvahikkunnathaayirikkum. Athu kazhinjaaludane first show Bhadradeepam avatharippikkunnathaayirikkum! Nazeer, Sharada, Sujatha ennivaradangiya kudumba chitram." ("Everyone please come, the grand opening of the much-awaited Sapna air-conditioned theatre will be presided over by the Trichur district collector (head of local government bureaucracy) M Krishnamoorthi on Friday sharp at four-thirty. After that, the first show will feature the movie *Bhadradeepam* starring Prem Nazeer, Sharada, and Sujatha, a great family picture.")

Shankaran grumbled, "With all that noise, it is hard to hear anything. All these Gulf people are coming back with more money in their pockets than they know what to do with."

Lakshmi offered to treat her parents to the movie, but they declined, not wanting to deal with the jostling crowds on an opening night. When her brother, Balan, came home after college and his usual jaunts with his buddies, it was decided that he should accompany her to the theatre on Friday.

He had wanted to go with his friends and was not looking forward to chaperoning his sister, but the look his father gave him brooked no further discussion. In the end, he sat down for a late dinner. While Nalini served his food, Balan laid out his conditions to Lakshmi: she should pay not only for his movie tickets, but also for a Fanta and a five-star bar of chocolate.

Lakshmi just shook her head and laughed at his impertinence.

When school ended on Friday, she hurried home and gulped down the tea and banana fritters her mother had prepared. She changed her sari, lined her eyes with kohl, brushed her beautiful long hair and partially braided it. In her household, going to the movies was a special event, and she was determined to enjoy every minute.

Brother and sister hurried to the theatre. Throngs of people milled around, waiting to get in. Lakshmi gave Balan the money for the tickets and he went to the ticket booth.

Lakshmi was waiting to one side of the main entrance when a police Jeep with its lights flashing pulled into the portico, followed by the state government's Ambassador car with the Indian flag prominently flying on its hood. The district collector had arrived.

She barely had time to register all this before her heart stopped. Stepping out from inside the theatre to greet the distinguished guests was the owner of the theatre and his staff members.

After almost seven long years, she saw the same disarming smile and mischievous dimples. He had gotten much thinner, his face was slightly more gaunt, and years in the Arabian sun had turned him golden brown. His lean, muscular body with its agile movements, were telltale signs of hard physical work over many years. In his gray safari suit, he was the picture of a man who had made it by the sweat of his brow and innate intelligence. He radiated an unshakable confidence.

The girl stood rooted to the spot, her eyes riveted on the man who strode forward to shake hands with the district collector and lead him towards the big blue ribbon tied across the entrance.

Around her, people pushed and shoved to make their way into the theatre. She was oblivious to all that.

Now the collector was speaking. "Nammude naadine ennum orthe kondum, ividathe ellaa kalaapremikale orthukondum thudangiya Sapna theater ennum ore vijayamaagatte. Idine vendi adwaaniche, kashe modakki ee swapnam saadhichedutha nammude priyappetta Shree Haneef Mohammadinodum ee jillakke vendi ende nandi reghappeduthikkollunnu. Ivide janiche valarnne gulfil poyi ore nalla companiyil ore nalla joliaayitte

CHAPTER 28

jeevikumbozhum nammale onnum idheham marannilla. Ende abhinandanangal!" ("This Sapna Theatre was started to give back something to this community, and to all the people here who love art. I wish this venture every success. I also want to thank the man who worked tirelessly for this and spent much of his money on this venture, Mr. Hanif Mohamed. He was born here and later went to the Gulf. Even as he climbed the corporate ladder and was rewarded with a great job in a reputable company, he did not forget us. My hearty congratulations!")

As the collector spoke, Hanif Mohamed stood next to him and scanned the crowd. Did Lakshmi imagine it? Did his eyes meet hers, if just for a moment?

She wished she had worn a better sari and taken more pains over her appearance. The next minute she chided herself—what difference did it make? He probably already had a wife, a beautiful Muslim girl, and a couple of adorable children.

Lakshmi strained her neck to see if there was anyone behind him. But all she saw were his usual buddies, Bashir, Javed, and the rest of the gang. That meant nothing. If his wife was a conservative Muslim woman, she might opt to stay at home, rather than be seen in a very public place.

Lakshmi's emotions were in a tangle; she barely registered Hanif Mohamed handing a pair of scissors to the collector to cut the ribbon. The theatre was officially open to the public. As the distinguished guests climbed the portico steps that led towards the main doors leading inside, Hanif Mohamed glanced one more time at the young woman standing motionless by the entrance. Lakshmi saw him whisper something to Bashir.

By then, Balan had returned with the tickets. He was beside himself with excitement. "Chechi, collectore ponathe kando? Ee thetere aarudeyaanenne chechikke manassilaayo? Athaa erachi vettukaaran Mammukkoyede mon Haneef Mohammadindeyaa! Kalla thoni keri Gulfee poyi kashindaakki vannadaa." ("Big sister, did you see the collector? Do you know who this theatre belongs to? You remember the butcher Mammukkoya's son, Hanif Mohamed! He went to Dubai on a smuggler's boat and made all this money.")

Lakshmi sharply shushed him and led the way towards the second-class seating entrance, because that is what they had bought. Bashir was standing at the entrance. Before they could present their ticket he smiled and said, "Athindeyonnum aavashyam illa. Mothalaali ningalke first-class seatingine erppaade cheythittunde. Angotte pogaam." ("Don't worry about the tickets. The boss has organized first-class seating for you. Let's go there.")

Lakshmi tried to protest, but Bashir would hear none of it. He led the way to the best seats in the house. Not wanting to make a scene, Lakshmi timidly followed. When Bashir left, she warned her brother that he had better not mention this at home. For once, Balan listened, remembering the problems he had caused her the last time he opened his mouth.

The theatre was magical. The seats were plush with velvet coverings, and the lights were subdued so that they did not hurt one's eyes. Although it was a head-splitting 95 degrees outside, inside the theatre it was cool and soothing.

The siblings tried out the different inclines on the seats, and giggled at the luxury of it all. Even the floor was carpeted. With a flurry of trumpets, the velvet curtains slowly rose and the movie started.

Lakshmi's heart fluttered. Was she reading too much into a careless gesture? Was it gratitude for all the help she had given him in the classroom, or was it something else? She could barely concentrate on the movie. At the interval, a uniformed doorman arrived bearing two Fantas with straws in the bottles and two bars of five-star chocolates that cost ₹10 each. "Mothalaali ayachathaa." ("The boss sent this for you.")

This was an unexpected luxury. Lakshmi had planned to spring for only a Fanta and a five-star for her brother, as a bribe for accompanying her. Her heart soared; even amid all the confusion of the theatre opening, he had not forgotten her.

At home after the movie, Amma had saved their dinner. She was surprised to find both her children non-talkative. Balan was subdued, Lakshmi seemed restless, and neither one was particularly interested in the food. Nalini was perplexed.

That night, as Lakshmi lay tossing and turning in her bed, she kept replaying the events of the day. Seeing Hanif Mohamed again had brought back many beautiful memories, and she realized how much she had missed him. His was a memory to be cherished in the heart, but never to be spoken or acted upon. Her practical mind reminded her that she was building castles in the air, and that is all they would ever be.

❉

"Lakshmi, schoolokke engane ponoo? Budhimuttundo?" Shailaja teacher inquired, still looking out for her favorite pupil. ("Lakshmi, how is it going at the school? Do you have any problems?") Lakshmi had continued tutoring at the teacher's makeshift classroom even after she got a job at the government school.

There was a connection between the two of them that neither wanted to break off. "Kozhappamillya. Pillere nalla koodiyathaa." ("Not too bad. The kids are something else.")

Lakshmi laughed as she took leave of the teacher. "Appo ini adutha aazhcha kaanaam." ("I will see you next week.") She started walking home. Her mind was still on the movie theatre and the man who built it. Seeing him after such a long time, the garden inside her bloomed once more.

She had never allowed herself to entertain the possibility of being together with him. It was a taboo she never crossed in her mind, even if in her heart she had transgressed many times. She was so preoccupied that when she turned the bend in the road with its dense foliage on both sides, she did not notice the green Ambassador car parked to the side of the road.

"Ippozhum enne polathe maramandanmaarke kanakke paranje kodukkalaa pani alle?" ("Are you still trying to teach mathematics to blockheads like me?")

Lakshmi was startled to hear a familiar voice. She looked up, and there was Hanif Mohamed, cheeky as ever, leaning against his car. Although every instinct told her that someone was sure to see them together and report this to her father, for once she did what her heart told her, even if it meant setting herself up for heartache.

"Sukhalle? Vellia aalaayi poyille! Theatere nalla kemaayittunde. Athinde agathe nalla sukhande irikkaan. Ushnam theere illa." ("How are you? You have become a big shot! The theatre is beautiful. It was so nice to sit inside. You don't even feel the least bit of the heat outside.")

He acknowledged the compliment with his usual nonchalance. He said it had been his longtime dream to start a business in his hometown. He was just looking for the right opportunity and, unexpectedly, the idea had struck him to start a movie house. He moved closer, and as he looked at her, there was none of the playfulness she had come to expect from him.

CHAPTER 28

His eyes were serious as he anxiously asked, "Lakshmikke sukham thanne alle? Njaan kaaranam kore budhimuttundaayi alle? Ellaam Bashir paranjitte arinju." ("Lakshmi how are you? I heard that you went through a lot of difficulties because of me. Bashir told me everything.")

He saw her eyes fill with the burden of the unspoken humiliations and broken dreams she had had to live with. Yet even with worlds separating them, it was still easy for her to communicate with the lively young man with the warm eyes.

Lakshmi knew that the answer would likely shatter her dreams, but she had to ask anyway. "Nikkaahine vannadaayirikkum alle?" (Have you come to get married?) He nodded and said, "Athe, ithavana nikkaahe kazhinjitte ponullu." ("Yes, this time I will be going back only after my wedding.")

Lakshmi's heart sank, but she plodded on. "Veluthe chomanna kavilolla vella Muslim sundarikkuttie Vaappa kande pidichittundaavum alle." ("I am sure your father must have found you a fair and beautiful Muslim bride with pink cheeks.")

As they leaned against the side of the car, away from the road and prying eyes, he moved closer to her, so close that she could smell his aftershave. With a twinkle in his eye he said, "Aah, Vaappa angane korache sramangalokke nadathi. Pakshe njaan paranju enikke milk chocalettinde nerathile neende nivarnne, muttu vare mudiyulla ore Hindu pennineyaanishtam enne. Athaaraayirikkum avo?" ("Yeah, my father tried all that. But I told him I was in love with a beautiful Hindu lady the colour of milk chocolate, with graceful long limbs and lustrous hair down her back. I wonder who that could be?")

Lakshmi's heart burst with joy and relief, and she playfully shoved him. He caught her and they fell against the car, laughing.

"Ore problem maathram. Njaanavalkke ore ezhuthe koduthirunnu ende manasilullathokke ariyichitte. Avale marupadiyonnum thannilla. Ezhuthe cheendi kalanjittidaavum. Enne ishtaanonne enikkariyilla." ("There is only one problem. I had given the girl a letter to which she never replied. She must have torn it to bits. I still don't know if she likes me.")

She wiped away her tears and told him what she had carried in her heart without even knowing it. "I think I always loved you. I knew that they would kill me at home if I so much as mentioned your name. We were both at the mercy of other people; it seemed like we would have no future together. No job, no money; what were we supposed to do? So I kept quiet and managed the best I could. But even during the worst times, in my heart you were always my place of comfort. I want you to know that."

His eyes crinkled as he put his arm around her. Suddenly, she was not afraid.

"I have so much to tell you about all that happened after I left Kerala. And I want to hear all about your life and what you had to go through. We have a lot of catching up to do. Let us go get some ice cream."

Lakshmi hesitated for a moment. The familiar demons—parental and social disapproval—reared their ugly heads in a last effort to prevent her from seeking her own path. But it was a fleeting moment, and, with a spring in her step, she got into the car beside the young man who had always held a special place in her heart.

CHAPTER 29

When they arrived at the small booth that sold ice creams, Lakshmi felt self-conscious. Hanif Mohamed proceeded to order. "Enikke ore pista ball, Lakshmikkendaa vendathe?" ("I will have a pistachio ice cream ball. Lakshmi, what would you like?")

Lakshmi had never had ice cream and did not know what to choose. She told the waiter she would have the same. When she looked at the prices, her eyes went wide. That must be why her father never brought the family to places like this. Not to mention the immodesty of women sitting in public places and eating food!

Hanif told her all that had happened to him since he left. He held nothing back. He also told her about his current situation, his job as site manager, and his prospects.

Slowly, Lakshmi started to feel at ease, and felt brave enough to tell him everything she had been through. The loss of her marriage brought no regret to her face, but when she mentioned little Anuradha's name her eyes filled with tears. She did not feel the least bit self-conscious talking about the dark hours after her precious daughter passed away. She could see the sympathetic spark in his light brown eyes.

"After my daughter died, I did not want to carry on. Nothing seemed to matter. My mother and grandmother were supportive, and I can't begin to tell you how much Shailaja teacher helped. She gave me a purpose in life. I would like to continue that work."

Lakshmi was amazed at her own boldness, but she was not prepared to give up something she had fought so hard for.

Hanif Mohamed understood and was quick to reassure her. "They are always looking for teachers in the Gulf. Especially math teachers; you will always find employment. I have no problem with you working." That was a big relief to Lakshmi.

Suddenly, Naaraayankutty, the marriage broker, stood before them. "Alla idaaraa, nammade Haneefalle! Theatere nalla kemaay-ittunde ketto. Endaa sukham athinde agathirikkaan" ("Wow, isn't this our own Haneef! The theatre is beautiful. It is so comfortable to sit inside.") Naaraayankutty had seen them in the stall as he was walking along the road.

He turned to Lakshmi. "Kuttiendaa ivide? Achanum Ammayum Anweshikkunnudaavum. Njaan veetti konde vidaam." ("Child, what are you doing here? Your parents must be looking for you. I can take you home.")

Before Lakshmi could reply, Hanif informed Naaraayankutty that he would be glad to take Lakshmi home. The broker's mouth was set in a grim line as he walked away.

Lakshmi looked at her watch; it was seven o'clock in the evening. She knew her parents would be worried. And she had no doubt that Naaraayankutty would make a detour to inform her father of what he had seen.

CHAPTER 29

"Nammukke pogaam. Loudspeaker ippo avide ettheettindaavum, vishesham ariyikkaan," she said. ("I think we better go. The "loudspeaker" must have gone straight to my house to give them every detail of what he saw.")

Hanif laughed at her anxiety, but Lakshmi was acutely aware of their separate religions that were oftentimes at odds with each other, mainly because of the people who practiced them with fanatical loyalty.

"Ee cheriya pattanathile maathram ithe vellia kaaryaane. Ividenne poyaale venda mishra vivaahangal logathil nadakkunnunde. Ithonnum vellia kaaryonnum alla." ("Only in this small town this is a big deal. Once you leave here, there are plenty of interfaith marriages taking place in the outside world. It is not a big deal.")

Lakshmi tried to hold onto that thought for courage as Hanif parked outside the gate of her house. Her father was sitting on the veranda, and Lakshmi dreaded what was to come. As she took off her sandals before climbing the few short steps to the house, her father's voice stopped her. "Nee evideyaayirunnu ide vare? Tuition kazhinjitte rande manikkooraayille." ("Where were you all this time? It has been two hours since you finished your tutoring.")

Lakshmi's voice trembled as she tried to explain. "Njaan . . ." ("I was . . .") Before she could finish, Hanif came forward and stood near the steps. It was he who told Shankaran, "Njaan Lakshmiye kalyaanam kazhikkaan aagrahikkunnu. Avalkum sammadamaane. Inne ende bharyaye nannaayi nokkaanulla saambathika sheshi enikkunde. Lakshmikke oru koravum varilla. Vaapenode paranje sammadippichittunde. Aadyam alkum edirppaayirunnu. Achanum njangale anugrahikkanam." ("I wish to marry your daughter. She wants this marriage as well. Today I am in a financial position to take good care of my wife. Lakshmi will lack for nothing. I have managed to get my father's blessings as well. He was at first against it, but he came around. As Lakshmi's father, we would like your blessings, too.")

Then, all hell broke loose. Shankaran's anger knew no bounds. "Ninne ingane vellondem koode koothaadi nadakkaanaa padippichekkane? Maanom maryaathem vitte perumaarumbo veettukaarude maanam kedathane patti vella chindayundo? Nee inganathe vashalatharam okke kaanichitte ini njangalkengane thala pokki nadakkaan pattum?" ("Did we teach you to go around with anybody in this immoral way? When you behave without honor and decorum, did you ever think about your family? After you engage in such vulgar actions, how are we to walk with our heads held high?")

He ranted and raved about the problems when women get too educated and think they can make their own decisions without permission from their elders. Lakshmi was amazed at how calmly Hanif Mohamed received all these insults. This gave her a renewed confidence.

Her father was on the brink of telling her she was not welcome in his house anymore, but her mother, who had been listening to everything by the side of the door, intervened. "Samayam kore aayille. Mon veetilekke chelle. Samaadhaanamaayitte aalojiche ellaathinum theerumaanam undaakkaam." ("It is late now. Why don't you go home. Let us think about this calmly and make a decision.")

Hanif Mohamed looked at Lakshmi. She smiled to reassure him that she would be all right. The young man said to Shankaran before he turned to go, "Naale mudal register vivaahathine venda erppaadugal thodangum. Ore rande moonne aazhcha pidikkumennaa avare paranjathe. Vere valla Hindu chadange nadathanamengile nammukke athinum vazhiyundaakkaam. Enikke Lakshmiye avalude Achandem Ammedem anugrahathode kalyaanam kazhikkanam ennaane aagraham. Pakshe athillengilum njangalude kalyaanam nadakkum." ("Tomorrow we will start the proceedings for a marriage license. They said it would take two to three weeks. If you would like to observe some Hindu ceremony in the marriage, I have no problem with it. I would like to marry Lakshmi with the blessings of her parents, but I want you to know that one way or the other, I will marry her.")

After Hanif Mohamed left, Lakshmi's father was still so outraged that he was on the verge of getting violent with her. But somehow, seeing his daughter's serene, confident face, he lost his nerve.

This was not the meek little girl he had raised, always so eager to please. Nalini got between them and prevented a bad scene. She served dinner and called everyone to eat. Her husband said he was not hungry. He sat in the veranda fuming.

So, the three generations of women—mother, grandmother, and Lakshmi—sat at the table, and tried to deal with the situation. Her mother said, "Kutty nannaayitte alojichitte thanneyaano ee theerumaanam eduthathe? Aazhamulla kenattilekkaa eduthe chaadanathe. Namukke avare patti yathoru nishchayom illa. Doore deshathe poyitte budhimuttukalundaayaa, njangalindaavilla rakshikkan, athaane Achande veshamam." ("Girl, have you thought about everything before you took this decision? Remember, you are jumping into a very deep well. We have no idea about them. When you go to these faraway places and if you suffer difficulties, we will not be around to protect you, and that is why your father is so upset.")

Nalini was amazed to hear her daughter confidently say, "Athine ippo njaan koche kuttionnum allalo Amme. Ende kaaryam nokkaan enikkariyaam. Pinne enikke swandam saambathiga sheshiyum undallo. Ammem Achanum, Ammoommem aarum veshamikkanda. Hanif hrithayam ullavanaa" ("But I am not a small kid anymore, Mom. I know how to look after myself. And I can earn my own money too. You, father, and grandmother need not worry about it so much. Hanif is a good man.")

As these discussions went on, the grandmother seemed a little detached. She was close to eighty years old. She had seen India gain independence from the British, and the bloody Hindu-Muslim riots soon after. She had seen women groveling at the mercy of fathers and husbands. With wisdom that comes from first-hand experience, she spoke softly in her raspy voice: "Innippe ide velliore bhookambam aayitte thonnum. Naale ellavarum marakkum. Athreyollu. Chekkan muslim aayaalum, nalla yogyan." ("Today you will feel like this is an earthquake. Everyone will forget about it tomorrow. That is how life is. Although the boy is Muslim, he is a good-looking fellow.")

Lakshmi and her mother could not help but laugh at the old woman's insolence. Her father, sulking on the veranda, heard it, and was even more annoyed.

Later, Nalini took a glass of warm milk to the bedroom for Shankaran, who had not eaten anything. She sat on the bed and coaxed him to drink it. "Just remember that he came looking for her after all these years, and after all that she has been through. Many men would have forgotten about their first crush. The boy has deep feelings. And in Lakshmi's case, who would want to marry a woman abandoned by her husband, and overshadowed by the curse of having lost a child? She will have a nice life in the Gulf with a husband and children, and she can even teach over there.

"Even if we must suffer some social consequences because of this, if it will bring her some happiness, we should not stand in the way. And who knows? Balan has not shown much promise as a student, and his job prospects might not be great. Hanif might be able to arrange a small job for him in the Gulf, which will solve that problem. I know our relatives will be angry with us, but we will just have to ride out this storm. And after a while, people will slowly forget what all the fuss was about."

Her father's mood did not improve the next day either. Shankaran had just returned from work and was sipping a hot cup of tea on the veranda, when who should walk in but the esteemed president of the local *panchayat* (district), Mr. Achuthanpilla himself. In his starched white dhoti and *kurtha* (tunic), with a long white *randaam munde* (shawl) draped over his shoulders, he was the picture of importance and social rectitude.

Shankaran feared that Mr. Achuthanpilla had not come with glad tidings. He put his head inside the door and instructed his wife, "Alla, Achuthanpilla saaralle, irikkoo. Nalini, ore glass chaaya eduthe" ("Oh, it is Mr. Achuthanpilla. Please have a seat. Nalini, please get the gentleman a cup of tea.")

The visitor did not beat about the bush. "Ningalude magal Mammukoyede mone kalyaanam kazhikkaan povaanenne, broker paranje arinju. Pillere inganathe vidyatharam okke kaanikkum. Pakshe namale kaarnnommare vende avare paranje manassilaakkaan. Ee vivaaham nadannal chelappo ore vargeeya kalaham thanne undaayikkoodennilla." ("I heard from the broker that your daughter and Mammukoya's son plan to get married. Young people will have these silly ideas. It is up to us elders to advise them about the right way of doing things. If this marriage happens, do you realize it could result in a religious clash between the Hindus and Muslims.")

Suddenly, Shankaran was incensed. "Athinippo njaan indaakki kodutha kalyaanom onnum alla. Avare rande perum praayapoorthi aayavaraane. Enikke pennine pidiche kettiyidaan onnum pattillallo." ("I am not the one who arranged this marriage for her. They are both adults. If that is what she wants, it is not like I can tie her down to prevent it.")

With a dire warning about the terrible consequences the marriage could set in motion, Mr. Achuthanpilla drank his tea quickly and took his leave. "Oraale thodangi vechaa, ini pinnem aalkkaarke ithe cheyyaan dhairyam varum. Appo ellaam kuttichoraavum." ("Whenever one couple starts this trend, others will be emboldened to do the same. Then everything will be an unholy mess.") He opened the small gate and walked out, onto the road.

❀

Hanif Mohammed became a regular visitor at Lakshmi's house. One week before the registration of their marriage, his car pulled up to their gate. Lakshmi saw that he was carrying several thick plastic shopping bags. Her mother and grandmother also came to the door, curious to see what was in them. They didn't have to wait long.

"Ende koottukaaran Ravi paranju, thaan enthoru kanjoosaane, pennine ore pudavem koode kodukkaandaano kalyaanam kazhikkaan ponenne. Ningalude edayile ingane ore chadange undenne enikkariyillaayirunnu." ("My friend Ravi told me I was acting like a miser by not giving Lakshmi the traditional sari that every Hindu groom gives his bride as a token of his responsibility towards her from that moment on. I did not know about this custom that you follow.")

In typical Hanif Mohammed fashion, he had decided to remedy the issue. The women's eyes widened when they saw the beautiful sarees worked in gold brocade, in eye-catching colours. When they opened the next bag, there were a couple of red boxes in felt. Inside were four gold necklaces, shining in fiery splendor. The women lovingly fingered them, exclaiming, "Eeshwaraa, ende maathram kaashaayittundaavum ithokke vaangaan. Ithreyonnum vendaayirunnu." ("Oh my God, this must have cost you so much money. You shouldn't have spent so much.")

Lakshmi and her mother were extremely grateful because money was always tight, and they had been fretting about what she could wear to her wedding. The few good sarees she had were old, and all her jewellry had been pawned to pay for her education. When Lakshmi looked at Hanif, her eyes shined with the love she felt for the thoughtful, kind young man who would soon be her husband. Although his eyes danced with mirth, there was also a depth of feeling that was obvious to everyone.

Lakshmi had gained a newfound confidence, and she teased Hanif. "Hanife, Ammoommakke ore pedi. Ningalude edayile randum moonnum bhaaryamaare agaamallo. Appo randaamathem moonnaamathem okke varumbo enne upekshikkonnaa Ammoommakke samshayam." ("Hanif, my grandmother is worried. She knows that in your community you can have two or three wives. She is already fretting that when you take on a second or third wife, you might discard me.")

Hanif Mohamed laughed loudly and was quick to reply. "Athe ivide oraale nokkeette thanne mudinje povaa, appozhaa randum moonnum! Pinne enne vegam kuzhiyilerakkaaraavum." ("Just looking after one is making me bankrupt, and you are talking about two or three wives! It will put me in the ground in a hurry.")

Everyone laughed, and Lakshmi could see that even her father, who was attempting to keep a stone face, was trying hard not to smile.

CHAPTER 30

L*akshmi's feelings were playing havoc with her.* On one hand, life stretched before her with incredible optimism and endless possibilities. When she thought of Hanif, even her skin glowed with anticipation and excitement. Every time they met (mostly at her house), Lakshmi felt she loved him even more.

This man loved her with an intensity new to her. When he looked at her with the crinkle in his eyes and smiled, flashing his dimple, she felt like a teenager who could melt into his arms. But she was also acutely aware of the immense gratitude she felt towards the people who had not given up on her, even when she thought she had given up on herself. They believed in her and wanted her to fulfill her dreams.

She was fully aware of how often Amma and Ammoomma had stood with her, many times incurring the wrath of her father. Within the narrow confines of their society, they had figuratively had to cross oceans to accept the enormity of Lakshmi's actions. She knew that her family had endured constant criticism and sometimes even estrangement from friends and relatives alike due to her actions.

She saw her mother wince when they went to the temple now, and some sharp-tongued lady would walk away, seemingly muttering to herself, but loudly enough for everyone to hear: "Iniyippo ividekke varanda kaaryam onnum illaallo. Pallee poyaa pore!" ("Now there is no need for some people to come here. They can always go to the mosque!") When Lakshmi was itching to retort, her mother would shake her head, and they would continue their devotions before the deity.

As usual, after his rounds at his new theatre, Hanif dropped by the house around teatime. Lakshmi surprised him with a request. "Ende koode ore sthalam vare varo? Valare pradhaanam aayittulla oraale kanaanunde. Avarude anugraham vaangikkanam." ("Will you come with me to a place? I need to see an important person in my life. I need to get her blessings.")

They went to Shailaja teacher's house. She was finishing her tutoring for the day. As the kids filed out, she came towards the couple with a big smile on her face. After having taken the bold step of bringing her future husband to see her mentor, Lakshmi suddenly felt bashful about introducing him.

But Shailaja teacher said, "Ee kuttie ithra sandoshaayitte njaan orikkalum kandittilla. Penne sundariyaayallo. Ketto Haneefe, kore budhimuttukale sahiche valarnavalaane. Athaanavalude shakthi. Theeyil kuruthathe veyilathe vaadilla. Ninakkennum nalla ore thunayaayirikkum." ("I have never seen this girl so happy. You look beautiful. Listen Hanif, this girl has gone through a lot of difficulties in life. That is also her strength. That which sprouts in the middle of flames will not wilt on a hot day. She will be a good companion for you.")

CHAPTER 30

Lakshmi basked in pleasure at these words from her mentor. Hanif spoke up: "Teacherine patti Lakshmi kore ennode paranjittunde. Teachere avale kore sahaayichittundennum paranju. Ellaathinum valare nandiyunde. Njangale anugrahikkanam." ("Lakshmi has told me a lot about you. She said you have helped her a lot. We are both grateful for everything. You must bless us before we begin our life together.")

It was what Shailaja teacher said next that brought tears to Lakshmi's eyes. "My blessings will always be with you. That goes without saying. As for the world, that is a different matter. People always say cruel things, but let it roll off your backs and pay no heed. I have read a lot, and I understand that unions such as yours from different religious and cultural backgrounds are not that uncommon in the more developed countries. You must give this little town some time to catch up with the rest of the world. Don't let people sow seeds of misunderstanding between the two of you. Make sure you communicate with each other, and even sometimes compromise, to make things work out. Go with my blessings; you have made my day."

Lakshmi marveled at the insight of the older woman, and she was also amazed how things that normally would have caused much tension moved so smoothly when she was with Hanif Mohamed.

✻

Lakshmi was watering her jasmine bush in the garden when she saw Divya walking on the road, holding her baby by the hand. Positive that she was coming to her house, Lakshmi opened the little gate and called out excitedly, "Neeyingotte vanno. Njaan avidekke varaan irikkayaayirunnu. Endaayaalum kore vishesham parayaanunde. Mattannaalaane kalyaanam.

Register affeesile vechaane. Appo aarem vilikkaan pattillallo. Nee vanne sareem aabharanom okke kanditte, edaa udukkandenne para. Ammakke ninne kaanumbo sandoshaavum. Adukkalele parippe vada indaakkaane. Kochu vaava veluthaayallo. Ippo kai pidiche thanne nadannolum alle." ("Oh, you have come here. I was just getting ready to come to your house. I have a lot to tell you. The day after tomorrow is the day of my wedding. It is going to be conducted in the register office so I could not call anybody. I want you to see all the sarees and ornaments, and I want you to select the one that I should wear. My mother will be so happy to see you. She is making lentil fritters in the kitchen. Oh, your baby has grown up. Now she can hold your hand and walk by herself.")

Divya did not smile and stopped for only a minute. What she said cut Lakshmi to the core. "Njaan ithrem ninne sahaayichathe ee vashalatharam kaanikkaan aayirunno. Enikke naanakkedaayitte thala pokki nadakkaan pattinilla. Bharthaavum, Ammem enne ende maathram cheethayaa paranjathe. Ini ee veettil vanne koodaannum, ninne kande pogaruthennum enikke thaakeedum thannittunde. Ithe Americayonnum alla. Vellia Mishra vivaahaam cheyyaan. Ippo sandoshaayille." ("I did not help you all these years so you can go and do something vulgar like this. I can barely hold up my head and walk in this town anymore. My husband and his mother gave me a real earful. They have forbidden me from ever coming to your house or seeing you. This is not America, where you can with impunity engage in an interfaith marriage. I hope you are happy now.")

Lakshmi was shocked to hear such venom coming from her best friend's mouth. Divya did not wait for an answer. She kept walking, and Lakshmi felt angry at the injustice of it all. She called after Divya: "Angane odi poganda kaaryam onnum illa. Ore mishra vivaaham aanennalle ollu. Veettee keraan paadillatha pole ivide aarkum vasoori onnum pidichittillallo." ("There is no need to run away like this. It is only an interfaith marriage. No one in this house has contracted smallpox for you to run away.")

Divya paid no heed and kept walking, leaving her friend fuming in the garden. Lakshmi realized with a pang that this was the first of many friendships and relationships that would be tested because of her marriage to Hanif Mohamed.

Lakshmi dressed carefully as her mother and grandmother fussed over her. When she was finished her grandmother exclaimed, "Endaa kutteede ore eishwaryam, nalla chandande!" ("My girl looks so beautiful!")

Her mother wiped away her tears with the end of her sari. Since it was not considered proper for female relatives to go to the register office, Amma and Ammoomma would be staying home.

Lakshmi touched the feet of her mother and grandmother and asked them for their blessings. As her eyes brimmed with tears, she silently acknowledged their abiding support and affection for her, even during the darkest days of her life.

Her grandmother's words were as much a prayer as a blessing: "Ellaam nannaayi varatte." ("Let everything turn out beautifully.")

Hanif Mohamed was waiting for her on the veranda. He was silent, but his eyes spoke volumes. There was an unmistakable light in them; it was as if he did not trust himself to speak because of the turmoil of emotions inside him.

At last, Hanif said, "Njangale vegam potte. Pathe manikkaane varaan paranjirikkanathe. Saakshikalaakaan Basheerinodum Raviyodum angotte varaan paranjittinde. Appo njangale poyitte varaam." ("We need to go quickly. They have asked us to come to the register office around ten o'clock. I have asked Bashir and Ravi to come there as witnesses for the marriage. So, we will get going.")

Meanwhile, Lakshmi's father could not take his eyes off his daughter, the beautiful woman in front of him. He climbed down the few steps from the veranda to the garden. Lakshmi touched her father's feet, and silently, he put both hands on her head.

Then, as Lakshmi started down the path, Shankaran called out to the man who was to be his son-in-law. "Mone, Haneefe, Basheerindem Raveedem onnum aavashyam illa. Njaan varaam saakshiyaayitte. Nalini, ore shirt ingotte eduthe. Namukke pogaam." ("Hanif, son, there is no need for Bashir or Ravi. I will come as your witness. Nalini, get me a shirt. Let's get going.")

Lakshmi looked at her father with gratitude and renewed respect. With one more glance back towards the two women huddled near the door of the house, she walked to Hanif's car. They saw him open the door for Lakshmi, as he had seen Westerners do, and they giggled.

It was a simple and sweet ceremony; more of a legal procedure than a ceremony. The officer in charge guided them through the process with practiced expertise. When they signed as man and wife, Lakshmi's hands trembled, and she saw that the usually nonchalant Hanif Mohamed took great care as he put his signature next to that of his wife.

With the formalities over, the couple looked at each other, and no one in the room could deny the depth of their feelings for each other. The man behind the desk and Lakshmi's father, coming from the old world, looked away in embarrassment, while Ravi and Bashir grinned self-consciously.

As the little wedding party walked out of the government office half an hour later, the afternoon sun was slowly climbing up the Western Ghat Mountains in the distance. It bathed the world in its golden brilliance, to heal and comfort humanity in all its frailties, as it went about the task of living.

ACKNOWLEDGMENTS

Growing up in Kerala, India, my family and I were all dimly aware of the illegal migration and gold smuggling trade taking place near Kerala's seaside villages. And as I delved deeper while researching this book, a fascinating world opened before me.

Several videos were immensely helpful:

- *Evolution of Dubai 1930–2019* and *Dubai Evolution from 1962 2021 Time-lapse* (Knight, Frank—Middle East), both on YouTube, gave me enormous insight into how a small, sleepy kingdom in the Middle East grew into today's mega-metropolis that competes on the world stage.

- *Gold Rush: Innovative ways of gold smuggling in Kerala* (The Federal); *Oman: Traditional Dhow boats under threat in the Gulf* (Al Jazeera); and *History of Safa Park, Dubai* (Dubai Tourism) were major sources that allowed me an understanding of the dangerous ocean voyages undertaken by desperate men in search of a better life.

- *Ben Anderson's Debrief on the Living Conditions of Migrant Workers in Dubai* (VICE/HBO) and *Deserted in the sands: migrant workers in the UAE* (International Labor Organization) shed light on the pitiable working conditions these migrant workers faced upon arriving on the promised shores.

I will be remiss if I did not acknowledge the help given to me by an extremely gifted young lady. Her talent for representative *and* abstract art has made her quite famous around Augusta, Georgia. Even as she pursues a career in clinical psychology, Vinaya Ann Alapatt still manages to find time to devote to her passion—art in all its forms, traditional and modern. When I approached her to design the cover for this book, she readily grasped the nuances and created a beautiful work of art that captures the book's essence. God has given her a very special gift.

Writing and publishing can be tedious endeavors, and the love and support given to me by my husband, Dr. Simon Sebastian, has been invaluable. He has worn many hats: as a cheerleader when I am riddled with doubts; as tech support to a very tech non-savvy wife; as the marketer-in-chief, coming up with innovative ideas to market my new book; and a warm shoulder to lean on. All this is accomplished in addition to a very busy career in psychiatry, which he enjoys tremendously. He is truly the "wind beneath my wings"!

As with my previous book, *Organic Tales From Indian Kitchens*, the help given to me by the team at 1106 Design was invaluable.

ACKNOWLEDGMENTS

My editor at 1106 was a great sounding board for the story. Her keen interest in the customs and traditions of 1950s Kerala gave me renewed confidence that the book might capture readers' imagination. I appreciated her attention to detail and her sympathy to the plight of Lakshmi and the many rules and limitations that bound women in Kerala at that time. Michele, Ronda, and Brian, you make what you do look effortless, because you have the experience to back it up and the success to show for it. ***Thank You!***

– Priya Mary Sebastian

ABOUT THE AUTHOR

Priya Mary Sebastian was born in Kerala, India. She received her bachelor's degree in English language and literature from Calicut University, Kerala. The author has been living in the United States for the past 43 years. She received an MBA from Centenary College, Louisiana in 1989. Priya Sebastian now resides in Augusta, Georgia, and has pursued her other passion- cooking, by operating a small restaurant for the past 18 years. As her cultural and culinary interests broadened, the author changed the concept of her restaurant from India Café to International Café', to embrace a greater world culture through food. She has always taken an active interest, and sometimes leadership roles in many cultural and charitable organizations. As an author, she finds the everyday human interactions profoundly interesting, and the strength of the human spirit when faced with daunting situations, nothing less than heroic! Her previous work "Organic Tales from Indian Kitchens" which came out in 2020 was a memoir/recipe book that gave a glimpse to the readers of what it was like to grow up in rural India in the 60s, and the food culture that prevailed back then.

www.ingramcontent.com/pod-product-compliance
Lightning Source LLC
Chambersburg PA
CBHW060354080526
44583CB00012B/304